VONU: The Search for Personal Freedom

By: Rayo

LIBERTY UNDER ATTACK PUBLICATIONS

Copyleft Notice

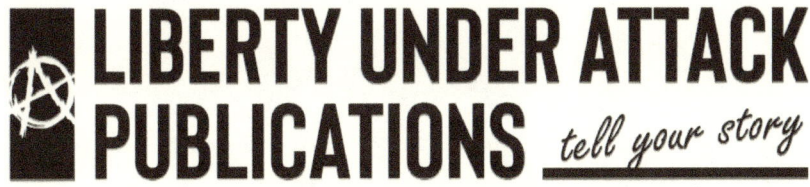

LIBERTY UNDER ATTACK PUBLICATIONS *tell your story*

Looking for your next read or listen?

1. **Adventures in Illinois Law: Witnessing Tyranny Firsthand** by Shane Radliff (Audiobook/Anthology)
2. **Adventures in Illinois Higher Education: Communist Indoctrination** by Shane Radliff (Audiobook/Anthology)
3. **An Illusive Phantom of Hope: A Critique of Reformism** by Kyle Rearden (Audiobook/Anthology)
4. **The Production of Security** by Gustave de Molinari (Audiobook)
5. **Are Cops Constitutional?** by Roger Roots (Audiobook)
6. **Vonu: The Search for Personal Freedom** by Rayo (Audiobook)
7. **Argumentation Ethics: An Anthology** by Hans-Herman Hoppe et al (Anthology)
8. **Just Below The Surface: A Guide to Security Culture** by Kyle Rearden (Audiobook/Anthology)
9. **Sedition, Subversion, and Sabotage, Field Manual No. 1: A Three Part Solution to the State** by Ben Stone (Audiobook)
10. **#agora** by anonymous (Paperback and Kindle)
11. **Vonu: A Strategy for Self-Liberation** by Shane Radliff (Paperback/Audiobook)
12. **Second Realm: Book on Strategy** by Smuggler and XYZ (Paperback)
13. **Vonu: The Search for Personal Freedom** by Rayo (Special Paperback Reprint/Audiobook)
14. **Vonu: The Search for Personal Freedom, Part 2 [Letters From Rayo]** (Paperback)
15. **Going Mobile** by Tom Marshall (Paperback/Audiobook)
16. **Anarchist to Abolitionist: A Bad Quaker's Journey** by Ben Stone
17. **Brushfire, A Thriller** by Matthew Wojtecki

Looking for a publisher? Drop us a line:
www.libertyunderattack.com

Dedication

TO RAYO, who walked this path before any of us thought of it, and to the freedom pioneers carving niches of personal autonomy in a world opposed to it.

Table of Contents

Foreword

Introduction

Section I: Theory

Section II: Practice

Additional Resources

Foreword

When I first picked up the little green booklet emblazoned with the words, Vonu: The Search for Personal Freedom, I was unaware of the significance of that moment. I was quite ignorant of the fact that this book, the one I was holding in my hands, would completely alter the plan I had for my life. I also had no idea that the response to this strategy would be so profoundly positive. Individuals (myself included) are seeking a way off the plantation. And that way is vonu.

"Vonu" is an awkward contraction of the words "VOluntary Not vUlnerable" and, simply defined, is the condition or quality of, as well as the action of achieving, an invulnerability to coercion. So, a vonuan is someone who makes radical lifestyle changes to become more invulnerable to the coercion of the State and the statist-servile society. These lifestyles include van nomadism, minimalist sailboating, intentional communities, country shopping (perpetual traveling), wilderness vonu, and sovereign free ports (i.e. libertarian countries), and more.

In Part 1 of this book, Rayo will walk you through the philosophy of vonu; in other words, what it IS and what it IS NOT. You'll come across a few, possibly new terms, namely controlled schizophrenia, political crusading, collective movementism, and the statist-servile society. I'll leave those for him to define, but the important part for future vonuans is this formula that Kyle and I worked out:

Political Crusading + Collective Movementism + Controlled Schizophrenia = The Statist-Servile Society

And the main enemy of the vonuan is the statist-servile society.

Rayo will also present some other interesting ideas; namely, some foundational definitions and philosophy, liberty at a profit, mean-time to harassment, the way to gauge the efficacy vonu, Rayo's presentation of the non-aggression principle in the 1960s, and much more.

In Part 2, Rayo will walk you through the practice of vonu. You'll learn about an abundance of possible lifestyle changes and even get a direct insight into him and Roberta's life as vonuans, including: what they had on their live aboard van, how they conducted import-export with the servile society, the methods they used to construct their polyethylene a-tent, his last known communication, and more.

In short, what you are about to read will be an introduction of sorts, a foundation from which to build.

You'll even hear the story of two van nomads, Karl and Jahla. They converted a Mercedez-Benz Sprinter van into a luxurious, functional, mobile "studio apartment," so they could chase killer waves across Australia. This will serve as a modern case study of the efficacy of this strategy – Karl and Jahla are definitely vonuans.

I also decided to add two original articles, one by Kyle Rearden and one by myself. This will give you an idea of how we are developing vonu into the modern day.

The book you are about to read was what initially inspired us launch The Vonu Podcast. It was the first stepping stone in what has now turned into a two year investigation that has impacted countless thousands of individuals, many of whom are pursuing their own lifestyles if they aren't living one already.

Since then, we've completed Seasons 1 and 2 of the podcast, and are currently on Season 3, wherein we are developing this freedom strategy into the modern day. Since then, we have received an abundance of new vonu/libertarian publications from the 1960s-1990s, which I then digitized and released for free in digital format. From those, we learned a lot of new information about vonu and have received further insight into the mind of Rayo, one of the most interesting freedom pioneers to ever walk this earth.

Since then, my entire life plan has changed; now, I see a clear path to a free future. No more, will I have to suffer through the exhausting 9-5 grind; no more, will I be relegated to "two weeks of vacation" a year; no more, will I be relegated to a life of, well, mere survival. Instead, I will do what it takes for me to be happy.

I am a vonuan and I will be free. And it all started here. Please enjoy, and always remember, vonu is yours for the making.

Shane Radliff
June 2018
The Vonu Podcast

Introduction

In the early 1960's a ferment began among some people who were interested in expanding personal freedom, and possibly creating a truly free society, one much freer than any that exists at the present time. This ferment, heavily influenced by the writings of Ayn Rand, grew to become the modern libertarian movement. One of the earliest libertarian projects was Free Isles, which was an effort by some southern California freedom-seekers to explore the possibility of founding a libertarian new country, perhaps on an island somewhere. One of the participants in the Free Isles project was a unique man who called himself El Ray, later changed to Rayo.

The Free Isles project never got beyond the talking stage. When it petered out, Rayo began looking elsewhere for ways to expand freedom, especially his own personal freedom. He decided that "land mobility" was a promising idea, so he moved out of his apartment into a camper mounted on a pickup truck. For several years he lived in his camper, and later at campsites deep in the mountains and forests, up and down the west coast of North America.

During these years Rayo wrote about his ideas and his way of life in several small newsletters and journals. The following chapters consist of a selection of the best of these articles, taken from Innovator, Free Trade, Libertarian Connection, and Vonu Life.

Sources

Innovator (called Liberal Innovator during its first year) was published from February 1964 to Autumn 1969, usually monthly. It was subtitled: "applications, experiments, and advanced developments of liberty." Innovator was one of the leading libertarian publications of its day, even though its circulation was only about 1000 at its peak.

Free Trade was published in March 1968 to November 1969 as a supplement to Innovator, on a varying schedule, usually bimonthly. It consisted of ads and unedited letters from subscribers discussing freedom ideas and applications.

Libertarian Connection began in December 1968, apparently influenced by Free Trade. LC was an "open forum" publication, which means each subscriber had a contractual right to submit a certain number of pages for each issue which would be published unedited just as they were submitted. LC was printed on mimeograph machine for the first 45 of its 6-weekly issues. Then a new method of printing was introduced, using photo-offset with 50% reduction (very small print). After issue #79, a new manager (non-editor) took over LC and changed its name to The Connection. TC is still being published as an open forum newsletter on a 6-weekly schedule. As of this writing, the latest issue is TC 110, which runs to 92 pages. You can get a sample issue of TC by sending $1.00 to Erwin S. Strauss, 9850 Fairfax Square, #232, Fairfax, VA 22031.

Rayo published Vonu Life himself, beginning in May 1971 until 1973 when he turned it over to another editor who continued it until November 1974. There were 17 regular issues of VL, and one larger issue called a special handbook issue, all printed by photo-offset with 50% reduction like the later issues of LC/TC. The last few issues of VL were actually called Vonu Linc, but I usually refer to them as Vonu Life to indicate that they were part of the same series. The 17 regular issues ran from 4 to 14 pages each. The special handbook issue, called Vonu Life 1973 was 32 pages long; about half of it was written by Rayo.

Prices

Since the following chapters were written between 1964 and 1973, the prices mentioned are very much out of date. To help you adjust the prices for the considerable price inflation we have endured since the 1960's and 70's, I have compiled the figures below. The second column of the table below comes from "What Would More Inflating Mean To You?" published by American Institute for Economic Research. It shows what the purchasing power of the dollar had declined to in various years, based on an index of 100 for the dollar in 1939. For example, the dollar was worth 35.9¢ in 1970, which means one dollar in 1970 could buy goods that cost only 35.9¢ in 1939.

I calculated the third column by dividing each figure in column 2 by the 13.8¢ figure for 1982. This yields a multiplier which can be used to adjust previous year's prices to see roughly what those items would cost at present (1983) prices. For example, since the multiplier in column 3 for 1967 is 3.0, an item that cost $100 in 1967 would cost about 3.0 times $100 = $300 in 1983.

When prices are mentioned in the following chapters, you can refer back to this table to find the multiplier for the year that chapter was written, and adjust those prices to see what their equivalents are in

1983 dollars. Of course, the prices of some items rose more and some rose less over the years, so this will give you only a rough estimate. But perhaps it will be somewhat helpful.

during year	relative purchasing power of dollar	to change $ amts. in this year to 83 $, multiply by:
1964	45.0	3.3
65	44.1	3.2
66	43.0	3.1
67	41.9	3.0
68	40.2	2.9
69	38.1	2.8
1970	35.9	2.6
71	34.4	2.5
72	33.4	2.4
73	31.6	2.3
74	28.4	2.1
75	26.0	1.9
76	24.6	1.8
77	23.0	1.7
78	21.4	1.6
79	19.3	1.4
1980	16.9	1.2
81	14.3	1.0
82	13.8	1.0

Section I: Theory

"The basic principle which leads a libertarian from statism to a free society is the same that the founders of libertarianism used to discover the theory itself. That principle is consistency." –Samuel Edward Konkin III, New Libertarian Manifesto

What Does "Freedom" Mean?

Is "freedom" a useful concept? Can a social environment be meaningfully described in terms of "freedom"?

Spokesmen for the political-economic status quo assert that man is, in large measure, a "slave" of his environment and his personal limitations and thus is never really free. This implies that acts or threats of violence inflicted on one man by other men are no more oppressive than are the misfortunes and restrictions inflicted on man by his physical environment; that, for example, a state edict to pay taxes or be imprisoned is not fundamentally different from the biological need to obtain food or starve.

If this view were correct, then freedom would be a sociological myth and all arguments for freedom would be empty phrases. A meaningful concept of freedom cannot include immunity from natural phenomena. A man is obviously never "free" from the principles of gravity nor "free" from the necessity of sustaining his own life (so long as he chooses to live.)

What is the significant difference between constraints imposed on a man by other human beings and the requirements of physical reality?

Man's physical environment is mechanistic; it is not volitional. Man's ability to function within his environment is limited only by his intelligence and knowledge and by intrinsic physical properties of the environment. Man may choose to increase his knowledge and devise ingenious ways to overcome apparent environmental constraints. And the environment continues to function in a potentially predictable manner, devoid of conscious intent. Man possesses and may use intelligence to alter his environment but his physical environment has no intelligent purpose to oppose man.

In contrast, constraints imposed on a man by other men can be the result of conscious, calculated, volitional intent. Purposeful attempts by a victim of force to regain his freedom can be opposed and negated by the purposeful counteractions of the coercers. Men bent on the forceful imposition of their demands can be a vastly more serious threat, a vastly more severe restriction on human action than are the non-reasoning forces of nature.

For this reason "freedom", defined as the absence of physical force initiated by intelligent beings, is a meaningful concept.

"Freedom" is a vital component of human effectiveness and fulfillment.

(from LIBERAL INNOVATOR, volume 1, number 4, May 1964)

How To Develop Liberty at a Profit

Initiated violence by government is the big problem facing humanity. Few libertarians will take issue. But why are efforts to achieve liberty so paltry, amateurish and inadequate compared to efforts to solve other problems?

Why must liberty be "marketed" so inadequately? Why is so little capital available for the development and sale of liberty? Government, much of it unnecessary and unwanted, seizes directly or indirectly about 40 percent of our earnings. In contrast, an insignificant fraction of our income is spent for cleaning compounds. Yet vastly more money is available for promoting new detergents than for all pro-freedom political and educational activities combined. It is therefore not surprising that new detergents are promoted incomparably more effectively.

Perhaps a "missing ingredient" is profit motive. One observes that new detergents are merchandized by profit-seeking corporations, whereas libertarian groups – political and educational – are dependent on philanthropic contributions in fact if not in name. (Unpaid expenditure of time to promote a course or book is as much a philanthropic contribution as is monetary donation. And merely setting up an organization which is legally "profit making" is no assurance of realizing profits.)

Can liberty be developed and marketed for a profit? Or are there crucial differences, which vitiate profit potential, between liberty and other products – between the elimination of systematic coercion and, say, the removal of dirt from clothes.

Existing governments are invariably "natural monopolies" within their geographical areas. An increase in freedom – a reduction in government restrictions realized by any means short of armed insurrection – potentially benefits every individual within the nation who does not seek the unearned. The benefits of liberty accrue to the individual whether or not he helps achieve greater liberty. For example, if a pro-libertarian is elected president and reduces income taxes, misguided persons who bitterly opposed the man, as well as person who did nothing, will benefit as much as those individuals who donated their time and money to elect the man. Is it surprising that the unspoken slogan of many libertarians becomes, "I'm all for greater freedom – provided someone else does the work necessary to achieve it?"

Each individual who does participate in a pro-freedom activity certainly will increase the amount of freedom or the rate of increase of freedom, at least slightly, and will thereby derive at least a small tangible benefit. But the benefits of pro-freedom political or educational activity within a nation are diffuse. The individual within a nation receives as tangible returns only a minutely small fraction of the improvements he brings. Most pro-freedom activity is a charitable donation to unknown strangers.

Are they ways for giving political partisans a self-interest in motivation? Yes, but the methods are probably not useful to libertarians. For example, instead of proposing a planned tax reduction program for all citizens, a pro-freedom candidate might propose the elimination of all taxes – but only for those individuals who contribute $100 to his campaign! Such a proposal would probably insure defeat at the polls. Further, such an idea – if it could be implemented – would almost certainly be found unconstitutional. Ironically, the pro-collectivist candidate can and does take advantage of short-range "self-interest" of immoral people by promising legal plunder to special groups and plunder-supported patronage to special individuals. Consequently, pro-freedom political forces labor under what must at least be called an enormous tactical handicap.

What is true for political activity is equally valid for most educational endeavors. Pro-freedom educational activities, of course, offer opportunities for tangible profit to a very few individuals such as writers, lecturers and professional staffers – who may be able to earn a comfortable living from their enterprises, but who could probably draw a much larger income working, say, in the advertising industry. And, besides, growth of such libertarian endeavors as book selling, lecture circuiting and institutional educating is, finally, vitally dependent on personal contacts by readers, followers and students – which are largely philanthropic.

The sparsity of personal, tangible returns constitutes a severe limitation on conventional political and educational activities, an enormous handicap to almost all existing pro-freedom organizations. The individual must properly live his life for his own sake. And he quite correctly devotes the major part of his life energies to those tasks which yield direct material profits. This does not mean that pro-freedom activities of the conventional sort are necessarily irrational. It does mean that such activities are largely philanthropic – little different in this respect from the Heart Foundation or the American Cancer Society. An individual can rationally participate in a philanthropic enterprise only if he judges his intangible benefits to be greater than his tangible costs.

What Pro-Liberty Activities will Yield Tangible as well as Intangible Benefits?

One potentially profitable category of action is tax minimization. If the individual can reduce the taxes he pays to the government, he not only directly benefits himself but indirectly furthers liberty by reducing the funds available to the government – funds which the government can use for vote-buying "spoils" schemes and propaganda in support of its collectivist policies.

Unfortunately, the amount of tangible benefits which can be realized through tax minimization is rather limited unless one resorts to illegal "evasion" of taxes or goes "on strike" and lives as subsistence levels – either of which may result in disadvantages which nullify tax savings.

A category of action similar to tax minimization is anti-inflation investment – holding savings in forms such as silver coins or stocks which have a commodity value rather than merely a fiat money "value." Besides benefitting oneself, such practices effectively reduce the quantity of government-issued money in circulation and reduce the ability of the government to plunder through the inflation mechanism of debt creation.

A promising new approach for developing liberty at a profit is being advanced by various groups who seek to initiate sovereignly independent laissez-faire free ports outside of the United States. It is proposed that commercial communities be developed on land sovereignly lease or purchased from existing nations. The major attraction of a free port would be complete freedom from taxes and regulations. For a great many businesses the disadvantages of remote location would be far outweighed by the advantages of total freedom.

Unlike the utopian community in Ayn Rand's Atlas Shrugged (Random House, 1957), which symbolized a withdrawal from the existing society, a sovereign free port would be very much a part of world commerce – though not of existing political states. The developers would not attempt to become economically self sufficient or socially exclusive. Many of the probable industries, in fact, would involve international commerce – industries such as resorts, warehousing, import-export, security exchanges and marine bunkering.

Investors in the initial free port development would directly realize profits through sale and lease of land. The land would appreciate in value both by virtue of being in a laissez-faire community and as a result of development. For this reason, free port development outside the United States would attract capital much more readily than can political and educational activities within the United States.

The secondary, social benefits of a free port would be impressive. Not only would the free port provide a political-economic haven for those seeking to establish a business, practice a profession, establish a private experimental community, or merely life free from state harassment – a free port would provide a valuable demonstration, a living refutation of the myths regarding the semi-capitalism of the 19th century.

To advance individual freedom, libertarians must devise unconventional approaches which utilize personal self-interest. The laissez-faire free port is one outstanding way to develop liberty at a profit.

(from INNOVATOR, volume 2, November 1964)

Some Thoughts on Libertarian Strategy

I have followed with interest the debate between political crusaders and self-liberators in Libertarian Connection and Free Trade. I make the following comments:

On terminology: Political crusaders try to categorize all non-crusaders as "retreatists." The "retreat concept," as set forth by Harry Browne and Don & Barbara Stephens, means disaster insurance – preparations to survive an expected future politico-economic disaster without substantially altering one's pre-disaster lifestyle. This is not the same as "self-liberation" – a change in life-style is not predicated on coming catastrophe. While a retreater and self-liberator may use some of the same techniques, their attitudes and general approaches are different. I am here concerned mainly with self-liberation.

Objections of the political crusaders to self-liberation – mostly innuendoes, ex-cathedra pronouncements and misrepresentations – have been refuted by me (Spring Innovator, page 7-47) and others. But the crusaders have consistently failed to refute or even acknowledge serious objections to any would-be libertarian political movement. (I am using "political" in a broad sense to include all efforts to take-over, replace or destroy an existing State through education, elections, and/or insurrections.) The two most fundamental problems of any genuinely-libertarian political movement are (1) its dependency on collective incentives and (2) the dichotomy between means and ends. Strangely, a free-enterprise economist, who understands that voluntary large-scale collectivism will not work in industry, believes it can work in a revolutionary movement. And strangely a revisionist historian, acquainted with many well-intentioned "reform" movements and revolutions which brought forth only more tyranny, believes that political activity can bring liberty.

Any realistic strategy must be premised on the real world. And explicit libertarians are a very small fraction of the population of that world. Whether this is due solely to cultural conditioning or to genetic inheritance as well I would not care to guess. But in any case, presently and for the forseeable future, only a relatively few people will have the intelligence, integrity and motivation to achieve or preserve freedom. The "masses" have the minds of serfs; while many do not desire slavery as such, their attitudes, customs and reactions constitute a milieu in which coercive governments can arise, and will; history provides overwhelming empirical evidence.

Hallbrook made the point (July Free Trade) that "the herd has never been on any side" and that "the war will be between the libertarian and the Statist vanguards." While correct, this is not very encouraging. For Statists have positive individualizable incentives for enslaving and plundering the herd whereas libertarians can only have negative collective incentives for liberating the herd. Libertarians will almost inevitably lose any such contest as they have throughout history. (For results of the American Revolution, read Ekrich's The Decline of American Liberalism.)

So any talk about continent-sized free societies, of whatever kind, brought about by whatever means, is strictly utopian. Such talk may be a pleasant diversion and may help "convert" the few who have libertarian potential. But in the real world, liberty will be limited for a long time to come to self-liberated individuals and (perhaps) libertarian mini-cultures and freeports. But this is not the grounds for pessimism or defeatism. One can forget about the herd and become free, once he exorcises the collectivist spooks from his head.

But while I reject political crusading as a strategy this does not mean I shun active resistance as a tactic. While seizing or destroying a State, even if possible, is usually worse than useless, selective-counter attacks may have value. In many ways a bureaucratic apparatus is like a simple biological organism. Pavlovian psychology is applicable. Cause a certain behavior (such as molesting a libertarian) to be "painful" and an agency will "learn" not to do it.

At first thought it seems that any conflict between an individual libertarian and a large State is hopelessly one-sided, but this need not be the case so long as the libertarian sticks to self-liberation and doesn't try to beat the Statists at their own games. While the State has much greater resources, it is a correspondingly larger target. The libertarian can hide or remain anonymous, striking at a time, at a place, and in a manner of his own choosing; the State cannot. Contemporary technology, if anything, favors the individual; anyone sufficiently determined can build his own nuclear weapon or (more appropriate for libertarians) psychedelic arsenal.

The self-liberator has tactical advantages over a would-be insurrectionist of any brand. The political crusader who wants to take over or destroy a State, seriously threatens the rulers and will bring strong countermeasures. But the libertarian who is satisfied to "co-exist" in protracted conflict with the State is merely an annoyance. The more-astute ruler is aware, as is the libertarian, that most people are sheep and will remain sheep no matter how the libertarian lives. Of course the Statist would still rather squash the libertarian if this were easy. So libertarian tactics must be such as to make counter-counterattacks ineffective and prohibitively costly.

One simple retaliatory mechanism is available right now to many libertarians: An individual puts part of his savings in a cache or Swiss account accessible to a friend and makes the following agreement: if he is arrested, so long as he remains incarcerated, his friend each month withdraws a certain sum and spends this for whatever will cause the offending governmental agency maximum annoyance and disability. (If the individual should be executed, all of his ear-marked savings are so expended.) This friend is contractually obliged to carry through the retaliation; even if the victim cannot stop it while incarcerated – this prevents possible intimidation should the agreement be found out. (This agreement is presumably kept secret.) The agency and the individual bureaucrats would, however, be told for what they were being punished; it would be pointed out the their victim was not only minding his own business but was acting in accordance with clear-cut moral principles; that he was not merely a "common criminal" – one of the herd gone astray. Through such a retaliatory arrangement the victim not only increases chances for release but gains a certain satisfaction; so long as he remains in jail, what better use could he make of his savings? (Whether or not such retaliation should be limited to "legal" activities is beyond the scope of this letter.)

Libertarians are devising many clever schemes for fouling up the State. But rather than applying these erratically and willy-nilly, I suggest they be reserved for well-defined limited objectives beneficial to libertarians. As retaliative capabilities grow, libertarians may be able to realize the de facto immunity from conscription, social security, travel regulations and other especially onerous violations of liberty.

Responding to Karl Hess' remark (Libertarian Connection #6): (1) I would not cooperate with the police in the apprehension of a libertarian revolutionist; anyone who did would be aiding the initiation of force and would himself become fair game. (2) I would be happy to shelter any fairly-rational libertarian revolutionist fleeing a State agent;

and, as suggested above, I might be able to offer him a more rewarding employment of his skills.

There is another area for mutual interest or alliance: ideological education. The revolutionary seeks recruits and the self-liberator seeks associates and underground traders. A specialist in educational services can profitably serve both.

A note to fellow self-liberators on this: Now that several good sources of educational services exist, I suggest a boycott of organizations which are knee-jerk hostile to self-liberation. This is not to suggest that educators must themselves opt-out or endorse any particular approach. But it is in our self interest to reserve trade and contributions for groups which (1) avoid categorical condemnation of self-liberation and (2) are open to advertisements of self-liberational media and ventures.

(from FREE TRADE, a supplement to INNOVATOR, November 1969)

Some Thoughts on Libertarian Strategy – II

Now that a collective-movementism (also called bullshit libertarianism and political crusading) has been discredited as a liberation strategy, it is appropriate to re-examine strategies which treat freedom as an individually-achievable way-of-life and marketable commodity.

I discern five general means of protection against coercion (initiated force): defense, deterrence, mobility, deception and concealment. Any system for achieving/preserving liberty will involve one more of these.

Defense: Defense as a major element of protection became ineffective with the invention of explosives capable of demolishing castle walls. Large scale defense became even more ineffective, and the State became obsolete as a protection organization, with the invention of nuclear weapons. Some defense means – firearms, karate, guard dogs, chemical disabilants, etc. – these are also kinds of deterrence – remain of some value against unorganized predators.

Deterrence: A system relying mainly on deterrence tends to be unstable and result in mutual destruction unprofitable to all parties. Its instability stems from the advantages of landing the first blow. One example is the "balance of terror" among nuclear-weapon States, which may break down at any time with catastrophic results. Another, more relevant to us, might be a band which camps *openly* (allows their location to become public knowledge) in the "National Forests," and tries to keep the bludgies (pigs) at bay by threatening to burn the woods. This might work for a while but would result, sooner or later, I suspect, in burned forests and imprisoned band members. As Black militants have shown, deterrence is valuable – perhaps necessary, but only as a supplement to other protection means.

Mobility: Mobility developed to a logical and useful extreme becomes international mobility or "country shopping." International mobility may be implemented by living aboard a yacht or out of a suitcase. Of course the "country shopper" does not achieve freedom from the coercive laws of States he visits; he merely maximizes his "legal" privilege – limiting his activities in each country to what is relatively unmolested there. In one sense, he is more "law abiding" than the natives in a port-of-call since he doesn't know the local "territory" – "law enforcement" practices and subterfuges – as well.

Indirect effects of increasing international mobility include, on one hand, a reduction of harassment by some small States which "compete for the trade"; on the other hand, intimidation of those States by larger powers (mainly U.S. and U.S.S.R.) intent on keeping their populace subjected. Ultimately the country-shopper's freedom depends on the deterrence/defense capability of his ports-of-call, as well as his ability to move from one to another.

Deception: Some libertarians hope to achieve freedom principally through deception. They propose to live "conventionally" in outward appearance while secretly conduction black/grey-market trade, designing protection devises (useful mainly against unorganized criminals), and enjoying illicit forms of recreation. I have seen many attempted free-market enterprises around Los Angeles during the past six years. And, almost without exception, these have failed for lack of interest/support or have been co-opted into something subservient to the State. (Telephone some "successful" private protection service and ask for help when you are molested by the big criminals). This lack of interest/support – the "psychological paralysis" afflicting libertarians, of which Natalee Hall has written so well, stems in part, I think, from almost continual vulnerability. Most debilitating is the absence of a secure home or "base" (mobile and stationary) to which one can retire to relax, eat, think and recreate. "Conventional" living libertarians seem even more prone to psycho paralysis than the populace at large, no doubt because they are more aware of the dangers. (Of course psycho paralysis is a subconscious evaluation; there need not be a conscious appraisal.)

One can practice deception 5 or 10 percent of the time, I think, without long term ill effects. But the "conventionally" living libertarian must remain on guard – must act the serf – almost constantly, day and night. (Bludgies prefer the witching hours for premeditated arrests). Even if the deceptionist escapes the cruder forms of harassment, he spends his life surrounded by a largely-hostile creature – bombarded by value-expressions counter to his own. The predictable results are neuroses and/or loss of convictions. One tends to become what he pretends to be. How many of the libertarians of even five years ago, who stayed in serfdom, are still active? Rational? Libertarian?

Clandestine free-market enterprise, with the development of specialized skills, will greatly enhance liberation. But this will flourish, I think, only among people who have already achieved a large degree of personal liberation.

Concealment: Liberation based exclusively on concealment amounts to two-directional isolation. And a complete absence of communication/trade with the outside world, while possible in the short term, would lead to primitivism and probably eventually to breakdown of isolation and increased vulnerability. Suppose, for example, that 100 years ago some small band had gone into seclusion, taking with them a good selection of skills, equipment and reference books of their era. Would their descendants now be capable of understanding and developing counter stratagems to aircraft spotting, heat detectors, nuclear fallout?

Strategy for Personal Freedom: An optimally-liberated life-style must involve a sort of one-directional isolation. The liberator maintains his access to their open-but-not-free trading centers while denying *them* access to his home. This requires a skillful blend of concealment and deception, plus perhaps elements of mobility and deterrence. A freeman obtains information, techniques, key equipment and supplies out of the Servile Society, exporting labor or products in return. And during import-export activities he practices deception – perhaps carries a driver's license ("genuine" or faked); perhaps pays some sales taxes he cannot conveniently avoid. But the freeman's "home base" is physically concealed. There he spends most of his time. There he may sleep, imbibe, love, design, build trade (with fellow freemen), and raise children in relative safety from the savages of State. A freeman's home must be a figurative castle.

In one sense, such a freeman cannot be completely free since his import-export is restricted. Neither would be a resident of a utopian "free country" who traded with someone in Russia – or Amerika. Import-export is easier for extraterritorial freemen than for residents of another country, since controlling millions of *square* miles of interior is vastly more difficult than thousands of *linear* miles of border. In either case, with growth, import-export becomes relatively smaller and more in the hands of specialists at "border crossing."

The liberated-home freeman, unlike the conventionally living libertarian, can segregate import-export from the rest of his life – essential for development of durable, growing, joyous, free mini-cultures.

(from LIBERTARIAN CONNECTION #14, October 7, 1970)

Some Thoughts on Libertarian Strategy – III

What is freedom? A symptom and perhaps one of the cause of psychoparalysis is the vague and evasive meanings given to "freedom."

Some libertarians consider freedom to be loosely synonymous with opportunity, choice or capability. This is popular among those who wish to pretend that they are maximizing freedom while they remain very much enslaved. Most residents of the Soviet Union are thus "freer" than a family pioneering on a remote island. Such a definition merely clouds. It is better to say "opportunity" when one means opportunity.

Others equate freedom with social morality – non-coercive behavior of others. They assert that "freedom" can only be bestowed by others, not achieved for oneself; that freedom cannot be achieved in defiance of threats since the very act of defiance represents a departure from what one's behavior would otherwise be, and is thus unfree. This definition also serves as an alibi for servitude.

What is a workable concept of freedom? I suggest: freedom is invulnerability to coercion, coercion being physical violence initiated by other volitional beings.

This definition does not mention threat of coercion. Any psychopath can utter threats against the universe. Threats are taken seriously only when readily implementable, which comes back to vulnerability.

Freedom is only one kind of invulnerability. Others include: immunity – invulnerability to a species of harmful micro-organisms – invulnerability to harmful weather.

One who continues in a vulnerable life-style and then complains when he is plundered, is somewhat like a West Indies resident who builds a flimsy house and then blames the next hurricane for demolishing it. Certainly, people are to blame when they inflict coercion. But merely blaming them does not bring liberty. The self responsible person builds a home which can withstand likely storms, and develops a way of life not vulnerable to likely attempts at predation.

No one claims that freedom is a summum bonum [NOTE: "the highest good", introduced by Cicero]. To achieve freedom one has to forego some opportunities and satisfactions while gaining others.

How much freedom? As Lee and Skye mentioned, freedom is not a monolithic entity; there are various degrees. But not all degrees are necessarily viable. For most people, I suspect that choice is between predominantly servile (vulnerable) life-styles and predominantly liberated (invulnerable) life-styles.

If satisfaction could be plotted with respect to freedom for a large number of people, I think the graph would have a low peak of relative satisfaction around 5% to 10% freedom, a higher peak around 90% to 95% freedom, and wide depression in between.

The lower maximum is exemplified in contemporary society by many a "successful" Middle Amerikan. He lives "conventionally" but takes advantage of some of the easier, more obvious loopholes. He pays income taxes but hires a tax accountant to maximize deductions. He registers for the draft but goes to college in hope of being made a technician instead of a target. His mental state is one of controlled schizophrenia. He believes most of the statist myths in which he was indoctrinated yet maintains a modicum of skepticism. He goes to church, or at least accepts their standard of morality, but is not "above" having a drink at a nude bar. He is largely rational in his work but keeps his rationality compartmented; he does not – dares not critically examine his life as a whole.

Although self-maintained schizophrenia leads to unhealthy and unhappy complications, on the whole the opportunistic serf may have it better than his more consistent, more gullible, less self-motivated brother who is drafted and becomes a target – and a paraplegic rotting in a VA hospital, struggling along in a low-paying, high-taxed job with a load of installment debts.

But the opportunistic serf is probably also more contented than the "non-conformist" who tried to be free in some things while remained servile in overall living pattern. One who is half-free and half-serf dwells in a psychological no-man's land. He knows too much and thinks to independently to play servile status games with conviction and success, yet remains too immersed in, and influenced by, that culture to achieve success/satisfaction on his own terms. This includes many (not all) "bohemians," "adventurers," black market entrepreneurs, religious/cultural minorities and radicals of all sorts. A half-and-half life-style tends to be unstable: some go on to more complete liberation; some drift back into, at first, outward conformity, then, acceptance of servile norms; some end in psychosis or early death.

The higher maximum of satisfaction is attained by someone with a liberated home-based plus some import-export with the servile society. For him, contact with the State is an occasionally annoyance and danger, not a big part of his life; thus he can avoid the psychological paralysis that afflicts so many "non-conformists." Compared to the opportunistic serf he may enjoy somewhat fewer conveniences (at present) but is happier overall. On the other hand, he has more than someone living in the primitive isolation presently required for 100% freedom.

Liberty or servitude? Or neurosis? Whether one will be happier as a freeman or as a slave partly depends on the individual. But this choice is not open to most libertarians. Relative contentment in servitude is possible only for those who believe in it; most libertarians are too independent and well-informed. For libertarians the choice is between freedom and neurosis.

What become of those libertarians of five years ago who gave up (or never tried) achieving personal liberty? Of people I knew, one is now a Catholic. Another is a Mormon. Another committed himself to a mental hospital. Many are occupied with chronic ailments.

Freedom for what? That is up to you, as Lee and Skye suggested. But in the immediate future I think most liberationists will include: freedom to pioneer in freedom – i.e. freedom to make a career of liberation.

At present there are no ways of self-liberation which are both easy and highly effective. Opt-out will become easier as more do it and develop techniques. But, right now, effective liberation requires so much of one's time and resources that one who does it will probably make it his main career – eventually developing services for sale.

Liberation is a many-splendored thing; there are various ways to do it and a variety of physical and mental activities involved. Liberation draws on a wide range of skills and offers many satisfactions.

To some, opting out evokes images of gathering berries in a far-off wilderness. Liberation does seem to be easier in uninhabited areas – at least as a do-it-yourself thing, which it necessarily is for the first pioneers. But it is also possible in large cities. Imagine, for example, an old expensive building, which appears to be only a private club, but which conceals an entrance way to apartments and workshops tunneled underneath.

Freedom does indeed "need" more full-time professionals; not collective-movement preachers seeking a coterie of followers, but explorers/inventors/developer of liberated life-ways.

(from LIBERTARIAN CONNECTION #15, November 17, 1970)

Thoughts on Freedom Strategy – IV (revised)

Freedom Terminology. In "...Strategy III" I defined freedom as invulnerability to coercion. But this definition goes contrary to traditional usage.

Funk and Wagnall's Standard College Dictionary 68', gives the clearest definitions and differentiations I have seen:

"Freedom, liberty and license refer to the right or opportunity to do as one pleases. **Freedom** is the widest term, suggesting complete absence of restraint. **Liberty** is a measure of freedom within restraints, granted by or as through by a sovereign power... **License** is an exemption from restraint granted to one person but not to another..."

Apparently no English word exists for invulnerability to coercion. "Sovereignty" comes close, but it is usually applied to States and implies not merely self-defense capability but power over others. This is not surprising since the very concept of invulnerability to coercion of individuals and non-coercive groups is relatively new, at least in European cultures. The traditional attitude is: rule or be ruled; there are no alternatives.

Roberta and Tom of Preform have suggested "vonu," which is a contraction of "VOluntary and Not vULnerable." "Vonu" is phonically distinctive; the closest words in major languages are German "von" (of, about), French "vont" (travel via), and Spanish "bono" (bond, script, voucher) – none of which means conflict. Forms of vonu and the corresponding forms of liberty and freedom are:

	Invulnerability to Coercion	General Exemption from Coercion	Absence of Coercion
Condition Of:	Vonu	Liberty	Freedom
Action of Achieving:	Vonu	Liberate	Free
Quality Of:	Vonu	Liberated	Free
Comparatively More:	Vonuer		Freer
Process of Achieving:	Vonuence	Liberation	Freeing
One Who Has:	Vonuan		Freeman
One Who Advocates:	Vonuist	Libertarian	
Advocacy Of:	Vonuism	Libertarianism	
Place/Situation Of:	Vonuum		Freehold
Art of Achieving:	Vonumy		
One Skilled At:	Vonumer	Liberator	

Of course, for all of these, there are degrees. Freedom is usually a **relative** absence of coercion (or of the effects of coercion); rarely is there no **possibility** of coercion. "Coercion" means physical attack (initiated force) against a volitional being or against his non-coercively acquired possessions, by another volitional being.

Vonu or Liberty? Vonu and liberty intergrade, as do almost all concepts in the humanities. Someone who builds his own impregnable island is achieving vonu. But what about his tenant who subcontracts protection? Perhaps the tenant is considered vonu as long as he remains able to pick and choose – maintains a high degree of mobility. But if he becomes quite dependent for protection, he only enjoys liberty with respect to his protector, although vonu with respect to outsiders.

How about someone working as an "independent contractor" rather than as an "employee" in Amerika, to avoid tax withholding? Superficially he seems to depend on legal loopholes – liberty. But tax withholding from independent contractors would be difficult to enforce so he enjoys vonu too. Two confidants who trade in secret are clearly vonu. On the other hand, employment with a "non-profit" corporation, which presently is required to collect social insecurity taxes, is only a use of liberty.

Is Liberty Undesirable? Liberty depends on laws and their interpretations, and so is easily destroyed. Vonu (while not necessarily illegal) depends on reality, not legality, and so is more durable.

Vonu and liberty interact in various ways. Achievement of vonu tends to increase liberty also; for example, the unenforceability of alcohol prohibition was a major incentive for its repeal.

Vonu also fosters other vonu. For instance, with development of a relatively invulnerable home-base (vonuum), one has more capability and confidence to engage in black market trade.

Large scale use of liberty, on the other hand, tends to reduce liberty. For example, the many men who remained in college to avoid conscription prompted circumscribing of college exemptions.

A large degree of liberty, long continued, reduces vonu. In the 30's, the American government was able to confiscate much of the gold mainly because of its long tradition of comparative liberty and relatively stable currency; most American residents trusted it and were unprepared to protect themselves from it. Similar confiscations in other countries were not as "successful." And American Indians were ill prepared to defend themselves against the highly organized forms of coercion introduced from Europe.

I suspect that any kind of "liberated society" is inherently unstable. In the general absence of institutionalized coercion, people will lose self-protection capabilities and become very vulnerable to institutionalized coercion – providing fertile ground for growth of new and (for a while) especially vicious States.

I doubt that products and services for protection against unorganized coercers would prevent this. A good mouse trap will not stop even a small bear. Nor will immunity to smallpox keep one from getting rabies.

In a sense States may be "necessary evils", necessary not to provide highways, mail delivery or other real services, but to stimulate development/maintenance of anti-state protection capabilities.

A state can be truly limited only by vonu – its inability to impose servitude and collect taxes beyond a certain amount; not by liberty – such as "constitutional checks" or a permissive king. A State which doesn't plunder as much as is possible within its social/technological environment, or which doesn't use the plunder effectively to perpetuate its power, will tend to be replaced, through political evolution, revolution or foreign conquest, by one which does. This is one of the reasons why political crusades to repeal coercive laws or have them ruled "unconstitutional" are a waste of effort – or worse.

This is a gloomy evaluation only for those who seek to evade responsibility for their own freedom. I am optimistic about prospects for increasing vonu. Vonu is yours for the making.

(from VONU LIFE #1, May 1971, which is a revised version of the original that appeared in LIBERTARIAN CONNECTION #17, February 10, 1971)

Some Thoughts on Freedom Strategy – V

Freedom through wealth? Some have said that the best way to achieve personal freedom is to first become wealthy. Here are some contrary points: Someone pursuing wealth tends to get caught up in associated status games and neglect his real objective. Psychological paralysis sets in.

Of freedom-seekers I have known who tried to get rich, most have not been successful, perhaps because they know too much to play the games with the same dedication and intensity as do the Middle Amerikan strivers. The few wealthy libertarians of who I know first became wealthy, then libertarian.

One is more apt to be successful, and perhaps even get rich, doing something he enjoys doing which he can do without contradicting his values, than he is doing supposedly high-income activities which he doesn't enjoy.

There are formidable and increasing hazards to preserving large wealth, once earned. Access to Swiss banks largely depends on government controlled mails, telecommunication and air transport. Caching large amount of silver is arduous and time consuming. ($50,000 buys a ton of it.) Also, the value of precious metals partly depends on industrial uses, and industry may not continue at present levels. Personally-consumable supplies, such as food staples, are the best form of saving. But storage and rotation of more than a few thousand dollars worth is formidable.

At present there is relatively little vonu to be purchased; it's mostly do-it-yourself.

Most high-income professions are narrowly specialized: dependent upon an economy of tens of millions of people. But only a relatively few people (thousands, at most) are apt to vonu themselves in the forseeable future; the demand in a small market is for broad skills.

Most of the relatively free people in North America today have relatively low incomes: "hippies," hobos, some Indians, some Blacks.

Historically, Jews have been more successful than Gypsies at surviving and maintaining heterodox cultures, despite their greater emphasis on wealth. (For what it's worth, Gypsies have enjoyed better "public relations".)

The emerging vonu minicultures will probably be more "tribal" than "capitalist" in form; invulnerability precludes large open markets.

There are already millions of people striving for wealth by non-vonu means. So let us develop vonu techniques and products to sell them.

Personal experience: I have only moderate savings; I'm not wealthy by most standards. But my achievement of vonu has been limited much more by time and personal skills than by money. There are many products and services which I could and would purchase if they were available; they aren't.

Of course someone already into a skill or business whereby they can earn much money easily may well be advised to keep at it for a few years and build a nest-egg. But, for most vonuists, I don't think wealth is worth much effort.

(from VONU LIFE #2, July 1971)

Thoughts on Freedom Strategy: Vonu/Activity Tradeoff

Occasionally, especially when some project isn't going too well, I ask myself: Can G and I achieve enough vonu for vonu to be attractive on more than an experimental basis? Or have we reached a point of diminishing returns beyond which a vast effort will yield only a small improvement? To conceptualize this better I made the following graph. The vertical axis represents vonu expressed in terms of mean time to harassment (MTH). Each vertical unit is approximately a ten-times increase in MTH.

The horizontal axis represents amount of activity; also difficulty of concealment. The units are:

•*Summer survival* – tent and bedding sufficient for sleeping, eating and reading. Occupants are one or two able-bodied adults. The occupants hole up; eat only stored food. The occupants come and go not oftener than once a season. Several months supply of food is on hand.

•*All weather survival* – shelter adequate for survival (not always comfortable nor convenient) the year round. Maintenance and trips are during good weather; only sedentary activities and minimal housekeeping are done during cold/wet weather. A several-years supply of food is on hand; there is no foraging. Occupants are able-bodied adults who come and go not oftener than four times a year.

•*Comfortable home* – Size and amenities are comparable to a small apartment or motorhome. There is one small family which may include small children or a non-able-bodied person. The people come and go not oftener than once a month. There is some foraging, hunting and gro-holes, but they live mostly on stores. They have no export products except possibly writing or art.

•*Small workshop or laboratory* – 400 square foot floor space. Electric power from water, sun or wind. And/or considerable cryptoculture. Frequency of communication to outside at least weekly; transportation at least monthly. Export products may include research/development, fabrication of small special purpose devices. One family, perhaps large, per site.

•*Small manufacturing* – of items with high value to weight ratios. Aggregate floor space is 1500 square feet (may be several separate units). Communication with outside comparable to telephone/telefax. Transportation at least weekly. Considerable export and/or purchases of most food. More than one family involved; perhaps two dozen people.

•*Light industry* – many products possible. Also, heavy fabrication for local use. Daily transportation. Extensive outside commerce. Up to several hundred people.

•*Heavy industry* – and/or communication/commerce center. Up to 40,000 people.

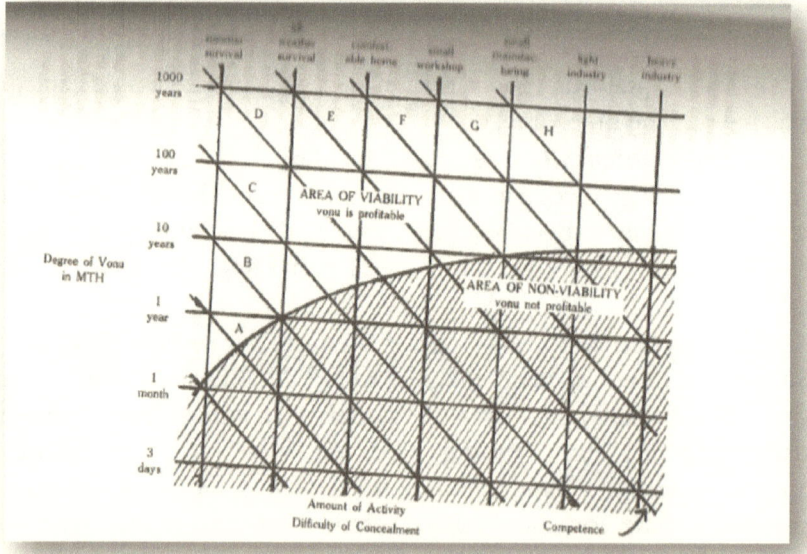

There is nothing immutable about this clustering of activities. Thus someone with only summer survival might have a clandestine radio link comparable to a telephone, while a group capable of manufacturing might still import almost all food. But I have attempted to cluster together activities which seem to be comparably difficult to conceal, with each unit representing a 10-times increase in difficulty of concealment. Thus, a camp and supplies sufficient for summer survival can be easily hidden, whereas concealing a heavy industry (such as a 'conventional' steel mill) would be extraordinarily difficult. Other levels of activity are intermediate in difficulty and concealment.

Within the shaded area vonu is not likely worthwhile – i.e. total costs of being vonu will usually exceed the total benefits. The boundary between the viable and non-viable situations slopes downwards to the left, at least under present conditions. This is because (1) the lower levels of activity require much less equipment and thus a higher probability of confiscation is acceptable; (2) the lower levels of activity are less suspicious and thus unlikely to lead to serious loss even if discovered. Thus a vonuan with only a summer camp will not look or act much differently than someone on vacation, and is unlikely to arouse suspicion if discovered. At most he will be ordered to move. Whereas a factory found deep in the woods (or otherwise hidden) will almost certainly be the subject of an intense investigation. Even if the operators elude capture, the equipment will most likely be confiscated. Almost certainly the factory will no longer be able to operate. If three years are the estimated time to amortize the initial cost of a factory (typical), the factory would not be built if estimated MTH is less than that. Exceptions involve illegal products with no non-vonu competitors such as drugs, with a very high profit margin and a correspondingly short time to amortize equipment costs.

The diagonal lines represent levels of capability one order-of-magnitude (10x) apart. Six years ago, when I was becoming seriously interested in vonu but had little experience, my competence was roughly represented by line A. Three years ago, after experience with living in a van, competence had increased to line B. Today our competence level is approximated by C. Thus, at present, we can choose among the following: a small tent, adequate for summer only, in a remote place with 100 years MTH; a larger tent and more equipment and supplies in a place with year-round access and a 10 year MTH (the larger tent is also more visible). When we want a home with amenities comparable to a city apartment we must move back to the van, and the best we have been able to do with it is one or two year MTH. If I needed a year around workshop right now, I'd have to rent space in a conventional building somewhere. Choosing a good situation and taking responsible care, chances are I could operate for a month before some bludg came around and asked to see my licenses (etc.).

With our present capability (line C) we really aren't able to enjoy a comfortable home the year around and be vonu. The price of living in a van is some submission to the bludg – maintaining a driver's license, paying attention to the legalities of parking in a particular are etc. With the van we are, in large part, enjoying liberty (legal interstices), not vonu. And laws and their interpretations often change.

So long as we have C-level capability we can trade off between increasing vonu and increasing activity. But increasing both requires more capability.

C-level vonu is attractive (except in a disaster survival situation) only to experimenters in vonu ('pioneers') who are interested in vonu for its own sake. We are somewhat analogous to experimenters with aircraft before 1910. These people built and flew aircraft (or tried to) not to get somewhere faster (trains were faster than the first experimental planes) nor even for aerial observation (balloons were more reliable) but simply to fly. Of course they anticipated future uses, but these would be profitable only after considerable experimentation and improvement. Someone would have been ill advised to build a plane in 1910 in order to (at that time) travel more quickly between LA and NY. Similarly our present capability at vonu has limited usefulness. Most people prefer a comfortable home that is relatively non-vonu to 'spartan survival' with relative vonu. We probably would too except that (1) we believe we can increase our capabilities, as we gain experience, to where we enjoy vonu and comfort the year round; (2) experimenting with vonu is, for us, an adventure – fun.

A minimum of D-level capability is necessary for vonu to be attractive to many people other than experimenters. E-level is probably minimum for development of much of an 'alternative economy' worthy of the name. How easily/quickly can we increase our capability by another order of magnitude or two? It is tempting to project past progress and assume we will keep advancing one level every three years. On the other hand we might be at a point of diminishing returns.

My present expectations are that G and I can progress to level D primarily by refining present techniques – living mostly above ground and importing most supplies. Progressing beyond D will probably require fully underground shelters and 'new' access techniques. (I'm more optimistic now (March 1973) than when I wrote this (November 1972). At mid-winter our plinu structure was doing well. And I've conceptualized life-styles which ease interface problems.)

Of course during the past six years we've made plenty of mistake which slowed us down; there was no one (we knew of) to teach us so there was much trial and error. Today we could probably guide an inexperienced but highly motivated person (what I was six years ago) to our present level in a year or less. But we aren't especially interested in doing so until we reach level D; level C is not attractive enough to justify a "recruiting/training" effort.

Vonuists disagree about whether one should first seek greater activity or greater MTH. Some believe that the neophyte should first try to build up a large and profitable but non-vonu (conventional) business, then attempt to vonu it. Evidence is inconclusive but I believe the opposite approach is much more promising: become vonu at a relatively low level of activity, then attempt to increase activity while maintaining or increasing vonu. Points: The more people involved and the more interactions with that society, the more difficult any change of life-style. A non-vonu enterprise is apt to have little in common with a vonu enterprise; experience gained during the former will probably not be particularly helpful when doing the latter.

Concealment is not the only means of being vonu; there is also deterrence and mobility. But someone who employs deterrence without concealment is essentially just a would-be rival State. Mobility is valuable only in conjunction with some kind of concealment or deception; if one can be easily traced and identified wherever he goes, nothing is gained by moving.

To some, deception/concealment seems so difficult or unpleasant that they opt instead for liberance – playing "legal interstices" while remaining otherwise "conventional" and visible. For myself, I'm not especially interested in liberance, partly because millions of people are already playing those "games" for all they are worth. I don't believe I could come up with gimmicks much better than what thousands of tax lawyers, accountants, draft advisors, etc. are doing. And "legal interstices" are transitory – as quickly as many people discover a dodge the bludg move in to close it. Of course a particular vonu way may not offer permanent security either; there will be new detection, and counter-detection techniques. But once vonuans get "below" the "noise level" of environmental change caused by animals, weather, and/or non-vonuans, the bludg and their detectives will be at the point of diminishing returns. In the short term certain forms of liberance have their attractions and are worth using. But I believe vonu has greater long-range potential.

(from VONU LIFE #12, May 1973)

Thoughts on Freedom Strategy: Utopias

(This is partly in response to the ongoing debate between advocates of "limited government" and "anarcho-capitalism".)

Both 'limited government libertarians' (LG) and 'anarcho-capitalists' (AC) believe in deux ex machina [NOTE: "God from the machine"] which will keep their idealized open-market capitalism pure. For LG the deux ex machina is a Constitutional Government which has powerful military/police forces to discourage foreign and domestic aggressors yet which somehow abstains from harassing the peaceful. For the AC the deux ex machina consists of various protection agencies and insurance companies, which remain peacefully competitive and cooperative on the whole, rather than fighting each other, forcing people to do business with them, staking out territories, and becoming States.

Both hypothetical systems are contrary to historical experience. Power corrupts sooner or later. State functionaries do what they can physically get away with regardless of what is written into a Constitution. A Constitution can be amended, suspended, "reinterpreted", or simply ignored. And, on the rare occasions when sovereignly-independent military forces have occupied the same territory, the result was not competition in protection but civil war terminating in one or more territorial States. Many AC seem to believe in word magic: if independent forces are **called** protection agencies and insurance companies, they will somehow abstain from doing the dastardly things which States will do. How insurance companies, for example, behave in that society as organizations subordinate to the State, is not necessarily how they would develop if independent of the State.

Achieving freedom and preserving freedom are really the same thing – States can be thought of as bad protection agencies (or whatever). But most LG and AC try to separate the problem of *achieving* utopia from that of **preserving** utopia once achieved. Few LG are seriously running for legislatures (other than for publicity) or testing the constitutionality of laws. Even fewer AC are attempting to organize protection agencies capable of defying existing States. Instead, to achieve their utopias, both LG and AC invoke another, higher-order **deux ex machina** – a "cultural revolution" – a fundamental change in the world-views / ethical values / political attitudes of most people.

Certainly popular attitudes can and do change, and can and do affect political systems. But LG and AC err in thinking of popular attitudes as something independent of and antecedent to a political/economic system. A person's world-views depend in large part on the opportunities and problems he perceives for himself; so long as he feels subject to the State and powerless to change it, he will rationalize that the State is really necessary if not good, and will reject out-of-hand arguments to the contrary.

I have come to question not only the LG and AC approaches to the problem of institutionalized coercion, but their ideal as well – open-market capitalism (which is not what is commonly called "capitalism" in that society). Even if pure open-market capitalism were achieved through some fortuitous circumstances, I believe it would be hopelessly vulnerable, both to outside enemies and inside power-seekers. U.S. economic and political history from about 1880 thru 1910 comes close to being an example of the decay of capitalism by internal forces (reference: Kolko's **The Triumph of Conservatism**). During that period there was considerable economic freedom and consequently relatively little stability of wealth. "From shirtsleeves to shirtsleeves in three generations" was typical. Large, long established companies were often cut down in a few years by newer, smaller, more capable competitors. There were no "safe investments" in which playboy heirs could multiply their wealth while concentrating on "high society" games. The "old rich" watched in dismay as "new rich," still with "lower class" manners and speech, enjoyed the trappings of wealth. It is no accident that many socialists were the no-longer-very-wealthy offspring of wealthy families. And it is no accident that many large industrialists were instrumental in obtaining government regulation of their industries. The supposed purpose of the regulation was to protect the Public from Big Business. And this served to co-op most of the "reformers" of that era into supporting the legislation. But the actual result of regulatory laws was to protect established companies from new competition.

There already existed a central government for the "capitalists" to manipulate and expand. But some large companies also hired private thugs to harass competitors and unions. If there hadn't been a State, it is difficult to believe that these forces would not have evolved into States.

Given pre-industrial technology, especially the communication and transportation which existed at the beginning of the "capitalist era," open-market enterprise, even to the limited extent it was able to develop under State controls, was probably the most efficient way of producing/marketing things. Given the vastly different capabilities today, I wonder if this is still true? Comparing problems of open (publicly displayed) market and vonu (clandestine) market: An open market is subject to State restrictions and taxes, if any, whereas a vonu market can largely avoid them. On the other hand an open-market can advertise openly, produce in large quantity, and sell thru a relatively few middlemen, whereas vonu marketing must be by "word of mouth" and requires either decentralized, small-scale production or many middlemen.

In the recent past, vonu marketing has been limited mostly to products and services which (1) can only be produced locally on a small scale, such as lawn mowing, auto repairing, hair cutting; or (2) are illegal. Products for which both approaches are competitive indicate the comparative costs of open and vonu marketing at a given time and place – e.g. alcoholic beverages.

In the future I expect more and more automatization of "word of mouth" communication and middlemen functions, greatly increasing speed and security at reducing costs. The newer electronic technology (integrated circuits) is greatly reducing the time/cost of coding and interpreting data. It is also increasing the ability of snoopers to snoop and correlate their findings, but not in proportion. For example a relatively small, cheap device can encipher data beyond the ability of any conceivable computer to break in a thousand years, or even to identify as a cipher. And soon there will be inexpensive radio systems capable of relaying data in ways not traceable by a hundred FCC's.

Here is how one such system might operate. To buy or sell something I type or speak an inquiry, order or offer into my Secure Communicator (SC). My SC enciphers my message and transmits it to SC's of a few individuals I know and trust, which in turn they automatically re-encipher and relay it in microseconds to SC's of people they trust, etc. In this way my message can quickly reach the SC's of a very large number of people. Someone who is selling what I'm buying has keyed his SC to watch for messages concerning that product. When my message reaches it, it deciphers and notifies its owner. He and I then converse, almost as easily as by telephone/telefax, but without having any idea who or where the other person is. At this time we may change our cipher so that our message is no longer intelligible to intermediate SC's which relay it. We come to terms and arrange delivery. If it is a physical product, delivery may be made through a drop. But most "products" will be information in one form or another, and can be delivered through the SC net. An example might be a program for my automatic micro-shaper which enables it to machine a replacement part for our home flour mill, or even parts for a newer, more capable automatic micro-shaper.

While a dishonest or unreliable person might join an SC net, he could endanger only his immediate contacts, who made the mistake of trusting him. Anyone who used the net to defraud could be cut out of it; furthermore, his immediate communicants would for a time be considered less reliable. My SC could automatically compute the reliability of intermediaries thru which a message comes, as well as selecting alternate routes. Proprietary data, such as a program for my hypothetical automatic micro-shaper, might be protected from plagiarism by putting individual variations of non-critical dimensions in each part. Payment would most likely be in credits, transmitted thru the net to an "underground" bank.

Secure Communicators and many other vonu products/activities will be developed and used only to the degree that people acquire secure shelter of one form or another, either thru outright concealment or by clever deception. SC's can be declared illegal, just as armored cars, firearm silencers and gold have been. All known abodes and places of business will be subject to inspection, just as they are now. And if an unidentified or "unauthorized" piece of equipment is found, the bludg will likely presume that it's contraband unless the occupant proves otherwise. Such laws will be difficult to enforce; SC's can be hidden or disguised, just as gold sometimes is now. But the few violators who are caught will be publicized. And most of those who lack vonu shelter will be sufficiently intimidated to abstain from using gold – or Secure Communicators. So vonu shelter is a crucial prerequisite for substantial vonu trade.

(from VONU LIFE #13, July 1973)

(Editor's Note: Ownership of gold bullion by U.S. citizens was illegal when this article was written.)

A Case for Non-Coercion Based on Rational Self-Interest[1]

The ethical principle of non-coercion[2] can be stated: One should not initiate the use of physical force against a volitional being or against property created or acquired through voluntary consent.[3]

Many people espouse this principle. But most arguments for it are mystical or altruistic.[4] Some are blatantly so; they invoke "God's Will" or "the Good of Society as a whole." Others are more subtly so, and talk about "natural law" or "innate rights" without clearly defining those terms.

Some supposedly-egoistic arguments for non-coercivism are merely reformulations of Kant's categorical imperative and thus mystical. One example: "If I deny inviolate rights of all others, I cannot claim such rights for myself."[5] A critic might respond: "My recognition of inviolate rights of all others will predictably have only negligible effects on what rights, if any, all others consider inviolate (assuming no God who enforces uniform rights)."[6] Another example: "I don't initiate force because I'd rather live in a world where most people don't."[7] A critic might respond: "I, too, would prefer such a world. But I have no reason to believe that my conduct will significantly affect the conduct of the world's population."

To base non-coercion on rational self-interest, what must I show? Only that I can expect overall benefits from adopting it – i.e. from espousing, internalizing and habitually acting in accord with it. I need not prove that coercion would **never** be in my self-interest. My decision to embrace or reject an ethical principle is not the same as my decision on action in a particular situation, although the former may decisively affect the latter. An ethical principle is only an abstraction, and like any abstraction, only approximates what it represents. Someone's conception-of-A is not A – a map is not the territory. But maps and other abstractions are often useful.

In rare situations initiated force may be in one's self-interest, and holding a non-coercive ethic (internalized as a habitual response) will mean loss. But this doesn't prove that adopting the ethic was irrational. [A]ny principle is adopted **prior** to the situation. The probability of overall benefit or loss, judged at the time of adoption, is what is significant.

Similarly, in some automobile accidents one is more apt to survive if not encumbered with a safety belt. But this doesn't prove that habitually fastening safety belts is a mistake. Overall probabilities of survival/non-injury are what count.

Most critics of non-coercion ethics espouse situation egoism, which is: Hold no general principles (except this one): always act according to self-interest as perceived in the situation at hand. Such a critic might say: "Why encumber yourself with principles? Why build spooks in your head? Why not play it by ear?"[8]

In reply: At any time I can consciously consider only a very small part of what is around me. I must deal with most of my environment thru habit and emotion. So the development of generally-appropriate habits is to my advantage. If I can walk over ordinary ground without deliberating about each step, I can better think about what is around.

An ethical principle, when internalized, becomes habits and attitudes. So the central question of this article reduces to: Is developing non-coercive habits and attitudes in my rational self-interest?

Consider the alternative: situation egoism. As each situation arises will I have time to deliberate? To the contrary, most opportunities to coerce are fleeting and require split-second decisions. Xerinye and Strakon[1] gave two examples. (1) You are one of the two astronauts in a space craft returning to earth. Suddenly you discover that oxygen leaked out; only enough remains for one man. (2) You are alone and see a big wad of bills lying beside an unconscious form in a dark alley. If one hesitates – in the first situation the other astronaut may strike first or barricade himself; in the second situation the drunk may regain consciousness or someone else may come.

In both situations one is apt to benefit from coercion if one acts quickly, without deliberation. But even those examples involve many considerations. In the spacecraft, more oxygen might be generated by electrolysis of water. Or the men can spend periods in drug-induced coma to reduce oxygen consumption. Even if no alternative to death is immediately apparent, a solution may be found with further thought. Might it not be wiser to chance this, or even to join in some cheat-proof form of Russian roulette, then to face possible revenge by the other man's friends and relatives back on earth as well as possible destruction of a craft in a flight? In the second situation: Is the drunk still unconscious? (Is it a drunk?) Might someone be watching from an unseen window? Might it be a trap, perhaps set by non-coercivists to profitably punish or eradicate coercivists?

Karate training emphasizes development of appropriate habitual responses. A combatant who tries to think thru each move is soon disabled. Similarly, someone who hopes to gain from coercion must not only reject principles, he must train himself to spot opportunities and act quickly, else he miss or bungle them. This is one cost of coercion to the coercer: time/effort/attention which could otherwise be devoted to other pursuits.[9][10]

A second, obvious cost is risk of defense or retribution by the victim or his friends or agents.

A third cost to the coercer is ostracism. He is not likely to develop close, long-term relationships with people he finds desireable. Even other coercivists would rather associate, between crimes, with those who are habitually non-coercive. Even if a coercivist is never caught – even if he never actually commits coercion, he gives subliminal clues to his attitude and habits thru gestures, expressions, inflections, mannerisms, and false starts. He may claim to be non-coercive, but in vain. Others will be uneasy when around him and will prefer to avoid him, although they may not always know why.

How serious a loss this is depends on his life-style and goals. If he prefers to drift around the fringes of big cities, forsaking close friendships, his loss may not be great.[11] But achieving freedom will be very difficult. Freedom, thru wilderness vonu, international mobility, urban hideaways and/or black marketeering, is enhanced by close, trustworthy confederates.

Many freedom achievers are especially sensitive to subliminal indications of attitudes and habits, because their freedom in part depends on spotting spies and other security risks. They, especially, are likely to shun a situation egoist. (How big a reward might be offered for information? How much could he rip off? Will he be tempted? Etc.)[12]

Conceivably a coercivists might become such a good actor his friends would never catch on. But this entails the greatest cost of all. He must constantly suppress, inhibit, fake – and live in fear of a slip giving him away.[13] I doubt that he can do this and retain a deep capacity for joy. And without it his 'successful' rip-offs will be hollow triumphs.

Could a band of coercivists avoid these problems by agreeing not to coerce each other, only outsiders? This is often attempted. Every State is such an attempt. But without a general principle of some kind, any agreement is without basis.[14] Some will turn on others the first time they perceive an advantage. And this possibility leads to distrust and sometimes pre-emptive strikes.

I do not claim that adopting non-coercive ethics is in the self-interest of everyone. But I conclude, that for myself at least and probably for most who seek to control their own lives, non-coercivism will maximize efficiency, probable safety, trade opportunities and emotional capacity.

AUTHOR'S NOTES:

[1] This article was prompted by and is in part a reply to: "Every Man for Himself," Krista Xerinye and N. Strakon, July 20, 1971, INVICTICUS.

[2] This is sometimes called the libertarian ethic. I now avoid that term because many who agree with non-coercion, including myself, reject other elements of libertarianism, especially its strategy and politics.

[3] This give rise to complex and controversial boundary questions such as: What constitutes force? What is a volitional being? What constitutes property, especially in the case of land and inventions? What constitutes initiation? But herein I consider only black-and-white cases of coercion/non-coercion.

With boundary problems, this seemingly-simple concept becomes very cluttered. I wonder if there is an alternative formulation (set of general principles) which handles boundary questions more neatly? (Analogy: Ptolemiac and Copernican frames of reference for astronomy.) But I don't think rejecting ethical principles is the answer.

[4] But altruism can always be resolved to either mysticism ("it is my Duty to (society, country, race, humanity)") or egoism ("I enjoy helping others").

[5] The Categorical Imperative: "Act so that you can will that the maxim of your action should be a universal law." To point up the equivalence to it (or to "The Golden Rule") and its inadequacy as a basis for non-coercion, consider a converse example: "If I grant to all others the right to rape me, then I can claim the right to rape anyone."

[6] Xerinye and Strakon[1] hold that "Natural rights is an invalid concept." Since 'rights' has religious and authoritarian connotations, I prefer to avoid the term rather than attempt to salvage it.

[7] But if "subculture" or "tribe" is substituted for "world" this becomes an argument based on egoism, since one can choose and be chosen by a subculture/tribe.

[8] I doubt that a situation ethics – absence of principles – is readily internalized. More likely I suspect, someone who claims this as his ethic is influenced by ethics (attitudes and habits) he has picked up from other people, especially as a child. It's easier, I think, to replace habits and attitudes with different ones than to simply drop them.

[9] Alternatively, he can choose a career in a form of crime (mail-order fraud?) not requiring split-second decisions. But this also involves much time.

[10] Some of these points were raised by previous INVICTUS articles responding to Xerinye and Strakon.

[11] As a potential friend or business associate, a situation egoist may be considered less desireable than a traditionally religious person who, while not consistently non-coercive, is at least fairly predictable.

[12] About internalization: Conscious conclusions about what I ought to do, strongly affect my attitudes but with a time delay of several years. Assuming as much delay in others, I would not expect a newly-avowed non-coercivist to act so consistently, and would tailor any association accordingly.

[13] This is also an argument against "conventional" living arrangements for vonuists and applied libertarians, which involve spending most time around hostile people.

[14] An association (and agreement) among a band of coercivists could be and often is on the basis of the general principle: One should not associate with anyone who has coerced him or his fellows (but it's okay to associate with people who have coerced outsiders). Such an association will continue only so long as anticipated benefits of future association exceeds benefits of coercion against a fellow. This depends on large part on differences between fellows and outsiders. The most durable governments and lesser criminal syndicates have been those different in culture or race from their subjects/victims. A wayward member could not easily/attractively "disappear" and find new associates.

A State invariably tries to indoctrinate its subjects, especially its lower-echelon functionaries, with either or both of the following beliefs: (1) The enemy is significantly different – not really human and therefore "fair game." (2) The enemy is really the aggressor; the State acts in self-defense. In either case the State is trying to invoke general ethical principles.

(from INVICTUS, December 1972)

(Editor's Note: INVICTUS is no longer being published.)

Section II: Practice

"Now that a collective-movementism (also called bullshit libertarianism and political crusading) has been discredited as a liberation strategy, it is appropriate to re-examine strategies which treat freedom as an individually-achievable way-of-life and marketable commodity." –Rayo

Self-Seeking: Free Isles

How can you increase **your freedom**? This is the theme of self-seeking – a continuing informal exploration of various ways for realizing greater personal opportunity in the present world.

The range of interest of self-seeking is the lifespan of its readers. **Self-seeking** is looking for approaches to freedom that will yield results within a few decades at most, and which will directly benefit the liberators. Likewise, self-seeking examines ways for living more efficaciously in society as it is.

To bring about general political-economic liberty is a formidable task. Most political philosophers have concluded that a radical change in popular moral attitudes must occur before freedom can prevail. Ayn Rand aptly summarized this in For The New Intellectual (Random House, New York, 1961): "The world crisis of today is a moral crisis – and nothing less than a moral revolution can resolve it."

But even the more optimistic prognosticators do not foresee significant economic-political fruits of a cultural revolution in this century; more pessimistic forecasts – taking into account the probability of further massive government intervention in control over education and communications, if not overt censorship – place results centuries away.

Long range cultural revolution activities are not, of course, to be deprecated merely because they will not bring freedom in our lifetime. Not only can an individual gain personal satisfaction by helping a revolution on its way, but a career in the education or communications field may bring tangible profits as well. The college professor in the humanities, the popular novelist, the writer of children's books, the advertising executive – each receives remuneration for his work.

When making career decisions the individual is, of course, primarily concerned not with the benefits that a cultural revolution will bring to everyone sometime in the dim and distant future, but with the benefits he will personally gain as a result of his work. And the course of action that is in the long term self interest of the individual is not necessarily the most effective for hastening development of new social customs. As an example, an acquaintance who recently graduated from college is potentially interested in and qualified for teaching high school literature – an excellent profession for constructively influencing developing minds. She has, however, chosen a position as a technical writer with an engineering concern – a position that offers much less opportunity to bring others to a rational libertarian point of view. Decisive personal considerations were: ease of obtaining the position, higher pay and greater personal freedom.

Are there ways to bring about a cultural revolution much more quickly than have been thought possible? Say within a decade or two ? The above example suggests that some mechanism for enabling individuals to realize an immediate tangible return from "converting" others, would be a potent "catalyst."

Attempting to vastly accelerate constructive cultural change is one general approach to freedom in our time. Another is the creation of localized areas of liberty in an otherwise unfree world. I have heard four different approaches proposed for creating "islands" of relative freedom. One of these is the "sovereign free port." Another is the "intentional community."

Described in March 1965 INNOVATOR, Preform's "free isle" would be a sovereignly independent commercial free port – literally a small new nation. While a "free isle" would be initially formed by and substantially directed by libertarians, it would be open to anyone who chose to come.

The most ambitious scheme for a local area of freedom so far proposed, a sovereign free port would potentially have much to offer. The "free isle" resident would (hypothetically) have all of the advantages of participating in world commerce while being free from taxes and regulations. Furthermore, a "free isle", if it were successful, could be a very effective demonstration of the merits of laissez-faire capitalism.

With such advantages go sizeable difficulties. Acquiring land for a sovereignly independent "free isle" requires a special treaty with a "source nation." A very substantial amount of capital would probably be required to interest the government of even a small, "underdeveloped" country in parting with some of its own territory. And the reaction of other governments to such a venture poses potential hazards. Preform now fears that economic isolationism by the U.S. and other States, if it comes, will annul much of the economic potential for a "free isle."

The "intentional community" is a smaller and more limited approach based on physical congregation of libertarians in a geographical area. The essential difference between an intentional community and a sovereign free port is admissions requirements – the intentional community would be smaller, less involved in external trade, not possess legal sovereignty, and require less capital.

The intentional community approach appeals to individuals who foresee an impending political-economic collapse and/or would like to try their hand at self-sufficient living. To others it might be of value as a vacation spot, or as a "bedroom community" where they could raise children away from many of the irrational influences prevalent in a philosophically "mixed" society.

(from INNOVATOR, Volume II, April 1965)

Self-Seeking: Green Revolution

"Ron and Laura became part of the Green revolution.

"The Green Revolution moves opposite to the Red Revolution – not bloody and violent, but quietly via persuasion and education. Not through government and the State, but through personal and family action... Wherever individuals, agencies and institutions – in Russia or elsewhere – distort and dominate the purposes and activities of other individuals, there the Red Revolution is active. Wherever individuals decide and implement their own purposes, they are part of the Green Revolution..."

Thus Mildred J. Loomis introduced Go Ahead and Live[1], an interesting potpourri of essentially libertarian views, information and ideas for realizing greater personal freedom through independence from the "cash and tax" cycle of State interference and expropriation.

In essence, Go Ahead and Live is the story of a young couple seeking a way to truly *live*, of their rejection of the coercivist status quo and their search for a more rewarding way of life. With the story as a backdrop and unifying theme, contributing authors present essays on diverse subjects – self-sufficient farming, home building, nutrition, child raising, education, sexual mores and economics.

To self-seekers, Go Ahead and Live is perhaps most interesting as an account of individuals who have tried self-sufficient living. It describes several "modern homesteads" ranging from a four-acre garden plot to a 160 acre farm and one "intentional community" of twenty selected families. All of these are within the United States.

"How much land constitutes a homestead? It varies with how self-sustaining you want to be," Mildred Loomis explains. "Perhaps you want only to supplement your city job; then an acre or two is all you need. Just enough to grow your vegetables and fruit, and possibly a few animals. Does this sound simple and insignificant? It isn't... What can bear some stressing is the relative freedom from exploitation on a homestead...You could... keep your cash income below a taxable level and still live very comfortably."

Martha Triechler adds: "It is not the size of the plot that determines what we call 'homesteading' – it is the emphasis, the values and the patterns of living you want to implement...We agree...that there are many political-economic errors in our society...We want very much to help correct them, and we do associate with groups and efforts moving in that direction. But in the meantime, we must live. We choose to beat the cost of living by producing more and more of our own. We do not do this because it is economically efficient...but because we enjoy it. Growing, storing and processing food; weaving, sewing and repairing clothes; making furnishings and furniture; creating our own arts and recreation – all of these are fun! Creative, enjoyable and satisfying."

Go Ahead and Live abounds with specific suggestions such as: "Start gardening with a small plot you can spade by hand. You can even start by smothering weeds and sod by covering it with a heavy mulch or compost pile for a season. Or pen a pig on the plot and let him root out the sod...Develop a vermin-proof storage room (or barrels) for corn, wheat, shell beans, sunflower seeds, and garden seeds...A cool, dry basement (or a cave dug into the side of a hill, or a pit dug in the earth and covered heavily with straw) will winter-store potatoes, cabbage, carrots, beets and celery." Ken Kern gives some advice on how to build your own home, and describes a house he constructed with a cash outlay of only $2950.

Don Werkheiser asks: "What is a libertarian community?" He explains: "One in which members are consciously and quite consistently self-regulative or non-authoritarian." A fictional community is described which is modeled after May Valley Co-op, Renton, Washington, about ten miles from Seattle. A dozen families formed an association, pooled their capital, and bought a 45-acre farm. Twenty half-acre homesites were plotted, the remaining land, including woods and pasture, was retained by the association. The homesites were leased only to families approved by the association. Fee for a 99-year lease was about $1000. Twenty families was considered optimum; large enough for efficient specialization of labor yet small enough to minimize costs of roads and water and to enable all families to know each other well.

The "total-sharing" community, such as Robert Owen's "New Harmony" and other disasterous experiments with voluntary communism during the 19th century, is discussed and gently but firmly rejected. There is "the need for persons to **individualize their interests rather than combine them. Persons who share goals can cooperate for certain specific** purposes...This is voluntary association and with it goes the right to disassociate."

Go Ahead and Live also includes some perceptive passages on education. "Something is radically wrong with education, and I think that error is authoritarianism. The State is coercive and most educators are doctrinaires. They differ only on what is to be indoctrinated. None are libertarians; much less do they believe that **liberty in education** is possible or would work. With rare exceptions, educators have been apologists, adaptors and rationalizers of the particular status quo in which they lived and operated. If we had liberty in education – if parents felt free to set up their own schools, or teach children at home – we would have a condition where the 'best would win.' People would choose which schools to send their children to. There would be a choice between different opinions about *how* and *what* to teach...This involves competition in education..."

Go Ahead and Live is not without faults. The more salient:

While a rational view of existence is implicit in almost all of the selections, there is not an explicit integrated philosophy – a serious deficiency in a book that would offer an integrated approach to living encompassing all essential facets of human existence.

A theory of interest is propounded which ignores rate of future discount. It detracts from discussions on economics.

The "organic" versus "chemical" farming dichotomy is entertained. Some of the dietary recommendations seem to be based on a mystique of Nature rather than a rational analysis of the actual merits of various food growing-processing methods.

One contributing author apparently regards love to be a cause rather than an effect of excellence.

Contemporary mixed American fascism-socialism is referred to as "modern finance capitalism" – an unfortunate choice of terminology.

Despite flaws such as these, I highly recommend Go Ahead and Live as a source of useful information for anyone who contemplates independent living. Go Ahead and Live also contains an extensive bibliography – of value as a lead to other sources.

The School of Living, Brookville, Ohio which authored the book, was founded by author Ralph Borsodi about 30 years ago. It is an information-education center for "homesteaders" and "do-it-yourself" individualists of all varieties.

[1]Go Ahead and Live, published by Philosophical Library, Inc., New York, 1965, is available from School of Living, Brookville, Ohio for $4.00.

*(*from INNOVATOR, May 1965, Volume II)

(Editor's Note: The present price and availability of Go Ahead and Live is unknown. To adjust the prices mentioned above for inflation, see the Introduction.)

Self-Seeking: Take Over a State

Two basic approaches have been previously outlined for creating localized "areas" of freedom – the sovereign free port and the intentional community. A third alternative might be called a "local congregation." A correspondent in Illinois (who prefers not to be identified) suggests:

"...a state could be 'taken over.' By 'everyone' moving to one state, a concentration of effort and voice could be obtained. A state like Oregon would be ideal; low population, varied topography and climate, coastal state for shipping, etc. There would still be federal laws, though, unless freedom was so well sold that the state might try secession."

He adds that such an undertaking should be executed without fanfare to avoid giving rise to conspiracy theories within the state. I would add that such an endeavor, by its very nature, might best be executed informally – as the net summation of many independent decisions by individuals. Central planning or direction would be prohibited by the number of people involved.

A local congregation may be either "inside" or "outside" – i.e. to a locality within America or to a foreign country. Possible objectives of a local congregation: achieve a complete laissez-faire society; secure a "base" for educational efforts; acquire local political control (though not independence); facilitate economic trade and information exchange.

Since most taxation and coercive interference with commerce is inflicted by the federal government, substantial freedom could not be achieved through an "inside" migration (excluding secession). But educational benefits might be considerable. The state-wide elimination of socialized schools would end one massive source of collectivist indoctrination – greatly increasing the number of people receptive to libertarian ideas. And a few rational libertarian congressmen could use publicity accessible to them for presenting rational ideas.

What state is the most promising terminus of an "inside" migration? The subscriber in Illinois presents the case for a small state – Oregon. I will offer an opposing view: In a large metropolitan center, although each individual has less influence on the state, a greater diversity of jobs exists, enabling more persons to come without economic sacrifice. Furthermore the larger cities are disproportionately larger culture centers, offering long-range educational advantages; for example, most network TV shows and mass circulation magazines originate in Los Angeles or New York.

My specific choice would be southern California, primarily because this area already has the largest libertarian population – perhaps a quarter or more of all the libertarians in the world. Unlike the Northeast or Middle West, a substantial part of the population is strongly pro-freedom – more important, most "rightists" in California are substantially rational and favor liberty not only in economics but in personal activities as well. For example, at least one "conservative" Republican congressional candidate has campaigned for complete freedom of speech and press – expressing opposition to laws against "obscenity," a stand which would be political suicide in most parts of America.

What about moving "outside" of the United States. Not for the purpose of starting a brand new community as Preform has suggested, but with the intent of locating in and eventually becoming a dominant influence within some small existing nation? How quickly could, say, one thousand libertarian activists alter a small English-speaking nation of 200,000 population? A few promising spots in the world are being studied with this in mind.

What location do you recommend? What are its merits?

(from INNOVATOR, June 1965, Volume II)

Self-Seeking: Ethical Enclave (Black Markets)

What is an ethical enclave?

An ethical enclave is defined here as voluntary transactions between individuals who are living under a collectivist government, when such transactions are conducted independent of that government. "Ethical" denotes the distinguishing characteristic of the participating individuals: an adherence to the ethical principle of voluntarism, the principle that no one should initiate violence or threat of violence against another. And "enclave" denotes physical emersion within a philosophically alien society. An ethical enclave is not necessarily a separate geographical entity.

An ethical enclave, by existing within the territorial domain of a coercive government is either legal – utilizing "interstices" in the taxes and regulations of that government, or illegal – operating despite threats of violence.

A simple example of an ethical enclave trade: A doctor seeks an architectural design for his new office, and the architect needs medical treatment. If either reports the transaction as income to government agencies, both are liable for heavy taxes. So they agree to exchange services in confidence, thereby realizing substantial savings. The actual trade may be conducted either as barter or in terms of a medium of exchange.

An ethical conclave may have similarities to a traditional "black market." But the differences are significant. The mixed premise "black market" operator, while violating socialist laws, still holds (at least subconsciously) some of the premises embodied in laws. He may experience a depressing sense of guilt; he may act with the handicap of psychological conflicts. The enclave entrepreneur, however, disavows not only the particular instance of initiated violence but the collectivist morality as well. He experiences an exhilarating sense of righteousness; he acts with the confidence and certitude of psychological consistency.

The enclave entrepreneur, furthermore, is dealing not only with immoral (by their own definition) "criminals" but with producers – with moral individuals who are committed on principle to hold confidences and honor contracts. His "costs of doing business" therefore tend to be less.

An ethical enclave potentially embraces many more products than black markets which deal only in illegal goods and services. In a nation where taxes and regulations are oppressive, a profit potential exists for trading in legal goods and services as well.

Ethical enclave trading profits participating individuals and promotes liberty in general by reducing the plunder available to the collectivist government – plunder which would most probably be used to finance further violations of liberty, plus propaganda to rationalize the violations. The potential effect of ethical enclave trading should not be underestimated. Mixed socialist government direct most of their extortions and regulations at trade – they tax primarily income and sales. But a transaction can easily be taxed only with the cooperation of at least one party to the transaction. Large scale non-cooperation would render income and sales taxes ineffective and greatly reduce government revenues – an ultimate check on a State's capability for violence against its subjects.

An ethical enclave would also encourage growth of a "libertarian movement" by adding self-interest motivations. Today many an individual who is implicitly pro-freedom is discouraged from gaining the knowledge necessary to become explicitly libertarian because personally profitable applications of such knowledge are so few. So long as the principle "profits" to be realized from promoting liberty are exceedingly long-range and indirect, few of even the most enthusiastic individuals remain active for any length of time; persons with a little less initial self-esteem simply reject an ethical view which they "sense" as "impractical," adopting instead the maxim, "You can't fight City Hall," which often becomes rationalized in time to, "Maybe the system is not really so bad." By offering opportunities for immediate personal profit, by rewarding libertarians for their intellectual honesty and perseverance, a thriving ethical enclave could be an unheralded but nevertheless substantial attraction for individuals of ability.

How might an ethical enclave operate? What is its potential in the present context? What are its problems and their possible solutions? To what extent do informal ethical enclaves already exist? What is the relative merit of an ethical enclave compared to other approaches to "freedom in our time"?

(from INNOVATOR, November 1965)

Self-Seeking: International/Sea Mobile

How can you realize the most personal freedom *right* now?

Become **internationally mobile**. Stop being a "captive audience" for the real life black comedies of a particular gang of clowns-turned-goons and begin making real market choices between States.

While no existing nation offers all-around liberty, many contain useful "interstices". So, the free-man-of-the-world, like the alert shopper who buys the specials at various stores, selects the best features of various States. And his very mobility gives added protection from the worst depredations. Elaborating:

In most of the States of North and Central America *except* the United States, the visitor is little molested so long as he remains economically uninvolved; so long as he only *consumes* (spends money he has earned elsewhere) and does not **produce** for the local market (secure employment or enter business).[1]

In the United States, on the other hand, one cannot **live** well – be it to establish a home, raise children or confidently engage in any long range endeavor. But by virtue of the comparative prosperity which yet remains (due largely to **past** freedoms), one can still **earn** with relative ease.

This suggests one mode of mobility: Become an "international commuter" who maintains a home in the Caribbean and makes occasional forays into the U.S. to obtain spending money. A person with a skill can earn enough in a couple of months to live modestly but comfortably elsewhere for a year.

International commuting is especially advantageous for the free marketeer who applies in his occupation the principles he holds. By minimizing both time spent and possessions kept in his "country of business" – the place where he is most vulnerable – he enhances security of self and home. Of course he avoids most of the taxes of his "country of residence," simply and legally, by not selling his services there.

While the economic benefits are significant, perhaps the greatest value of the home away from work is psychological. Safety within the Grave Society depends on conformity and anonymity; one must avoid overt expressions of individuality – take pains to blend with the grey multitude. But self-esteem seeks outlet in celebration. And the fruits of one's labors are best enjoyed far from the eyes of interested tax thieves and other people molesters.

However, in the long range, a **fixed** residence is unsafe *anywhere*. The coercive State – a maelstrom of violent interference – is inherently unstable; the relatively placid Banana Republic of today may be a nasty little despotism in a few years. So the far-sighted global gypsy seeks not only physical separation of work and home, but mobility of home as well.

One excellent way to combine the advantages of "permanent" residence with mobility is by making home aboard a boat. With the development of molded fiberglass hulls and synthetic fiber rigging and sails, yachts are becoming less expensive and easier to maintain; already comparing not too unfavorably with land-based dwellings of the same size.[2]

As more libertarians take to the water, some will doubtless anchor and migrate more or less together as a semi-permanent water-borne "community," saving time and money through the exchange of services – "internal" free trade not subject to the scrutiny of any State.[3]

The voluntary floating association has some advantages over the free-hamlet-in-the-hills. Not only will anchors be lowered where State interference is minimal; the very mobility discourages intervention. For instance, State school officials seldom molest the children of transients. Another blessing for parents: the irrationalist-coercivist influence of "outside" peer groups and mass communication media is considerably reduced. Differences of objective and conflicts of personality, which may disrupt an immobile intentional community, are easily resolved; the dissenters weigh anchor.[4] And a "community" can develop by easy steps and without formal direction; no would-be founder need acquire a large tract of land, uncertain as to market demand or the response of the State. The floating voluntary society beings with a population of one.[5]

The mobile libertarian not only bypasses most existing State coercion, but is well equipped to escape incipient totalitarianism. With the American government readying plans for general forced labor, rationing and censorship in the event of war or other "national emergency," escape can be essential for philosophical if not physical survival. And while a retreat in the boondocks can serve as a temporary hideout, when total fascist-socialism comes, those who fare best are usually those who leave early.[6]

While international mobility is a way to increase personal freedom, precisely for this reason it becomes an effective strategy for societal liberation. The mobile libertarian is **actively**, not just potentially, in the market for liberty, and any growing market tends to attract caterers. As more seekers of freedom cease their Sisyphean Labors of reforming particular governments and/or "living" with coercion, and become "country shoppers," a few ministate rulers may begin to "compete for their trade."[7]

How can you increase your mobility?

- **Learn more about foreign lands, and oceans**. Study the literature. Learn to sail. Learn a second language. Spend vacations traveling abroad.

- **Be mobile in occupation**. Avoid professions which require long-term fixed resident or extreme specialization. Consider instead:

  o Jobs involving travel, the ocean, and/or boats. The fisherman or charter-boat operator is already afloat and knowledgeable of the sea.

  o Independent intellectual activities. Many writers, artists, inventors and researchers do their work almost anywhere.

  o Temporary skilled employment. The "job shopping" engineer, designer or technician not only commands a higher wage rate than his "permanently employed" counterpart, but can be gone for months or years between jobs.

  o Migrant labor. Harvest workers can not only earn relatively high wages on a piece-work basis, but can usually arrange to take their pay in produce (which they may resell), avoiding taxes.

  o Service to other sea-mobiles. As floating "communities" grow, medical, educational and repair skills will be in demand.

If you are already established in a business which precludes extensive travel, economize, maximize short term income and save toward financial independence.

- **Secure your savings**. Choose investments which need little supervision and which are safe from State interference.

Internationally diversify while funds are still easily removed from the U.S.

- **Limit possessions to what you can move, discard or cache**. For housing, choose a yacht over a house. Or if you prefer to live on dry land, rent. For land transportation use a motorcycle, an old jalopy, or rented vehicles.
- **Base your self-esteem on extraterritorial pursuits**. If your present occupation depends on the coerced society, avoid ego involvement. Develop active interests which can accompany you wherever you go. Take delight in a panorama of new places, not in the minutiae of a particular locale.
- **Seek friends who are going your way**. Cultivate long term relations with libertarians having similar aspirations: potential neighbors in a future floating society.
- **Get a passport**, but don't depend on it; passports may be revoked in the event of a "national emergency."
- **Live at peace in a place of refuge**. If you wish to battle a State through political agitation or overt civil disobedience, fight where you "know the territory" – in your "native land" or a country picked with that in mind. But when you seek a "haven from the storm," quietly comply with or bypass local laws. If your State of anchorage becomes intolerable, don't waste energy in extended public criticism or conflict; apply your free market principles by setting sail for sunnier waters.

[1] Of course coercion directed against production is the main cause of "underdevelopment." But this need not be a primary concern of the perpetual "visitor" who intends to remain uninvolved with the local State.

[2] Several acquaintances have recommend trimarans for ocean living. Trimarans provide more interior space-per-cost, faster cruising, less heel, and easier beaching (important in unsettled areas) than comparable monohulls. Reportedly, a 35-foot "lodestar," which has the living space of a small apartment, can be purchased fully equipped in Taiwan for about $8,000. Sail-away prices in the Orient are little more than one-half of U.S. prices; of course the import duty must be avoided (possibly through foreign registration) to realize the full saving.

[3] See *Ocean Freedom*, a newsletter-notebook-forum on libertarian marine ventures published through Agoric Communications. Also see

"The Permanent Floating Voluntary Society" series by Kerry Thornley, July through December 1966 INNOVATOR.

[4] In the floating voluntary society, physical mobility may provide an effective defense against coercers, domestic or foreign. Imagine the frustration of some obnoxious would-be Mayor who awakens one morning to find that most of "his city" has left during the night. Or the chagrin of the Naval Commander who steams to the attack – only to be confronted by empty ocean as myriad small craft and floating structures scatter in every direction. A State, which is basically an institution for seizing **fixed** property (including mineral resources of the ocean **floor**), will be relatively incapable of inflicting injury in a society where people and most property are highly mobile.

[5] Looking ahead: As ocean dwellers proliferate, entrepreneurs will locate floating breakwaters outside of territorial waters and start floating free cities – the lure of laissez-faire attracting at first tourist business and later an increasing diversity of industry and commerce.

[6] To appreciate the difficulties of long term survival in the fully developed slave state, read The Diary of a Young Girl (Anne Frank) and Doctor Zhivago.

Of course, domestic fascism will probably be accompanied by more coercive isolationism – exchange controls and travel restrictions – as the rulers try to shift the consequences of their past interventions to innocent subjects. But if/when an American "iron curtain" is erected, I prefer to be on the outside looking in.

[7] With the large number of newly emerging ministates throughout the world, why has no country yet come close to true freedom? While irrationalist-coercivist mass indoctrination, plunder schemes of indigenous State officials, and American "foreign aid" programs deserve much of the blame, the decisive factor has probably been little appreciation for real liberty by those most "in the market" – businessmen dealing in international commerce. Significantly, specific freedoms which have been in substantial demand, such as free banking, low-cost registration and duty-free transshipping, have attracted "vendors."

(from INNOVATOR, March 1967)

Editor's Notes:

Regarding note 2, trimarans also have offsetting disadvantages, and heated discussions have taken place in sailing circles among proponents of tris vs. monos. Although typical recent prices of trimarans are not available, adjusting the price of $8,000 in 1967 for inflation would give a price of about $24,000 by 1982. Monohulls, of course, will have increased in price similarly.

Regarding note 3, Ocean Freedom/Ocean Living was published from March 1967 to October 1970. The first three issues were called Ocean Freedom, then the name was changed to Ocean Living. In all, twelve issues were published. Back issues are no longer available.

Letter From a Nomad

I am living in Big Tujunga Canyon. Bright sunlight and fresh air stream into my home. A hundred yards away rushes the creek. Beyond rise rugged hills, green with winter grass and budding shrubs. A few more days I will live here – writing, installing some equipment; then move to Los Angeles for a short, intense contract job. Next summer, when Tujunga Canyon is no longer very green and Los Angeles may be hot in more ways than one, I will be living somewhere in Canada. My home is a housecar.

I chose this way to freedom because it offers me the best of two worlds. I can live most-of-the-time away from regimented, congested, indefensible cities yet still profit by "exporting" my labor into these cities. I have the freedom and security offered by mobility; yet I possess what is in most respects a permanent residence. I can fully enjoy my life right now, yet live economically and accumulate capital for further ventures. Finally, I can "opt out" alone; while I look forward to trade with others who may choose similar or complimentary ways of life, my liberty does not depend on their decisions.

I am also delighted with unforeseen "fringe benefits"; ease of washing or resting after a journey; no worry about what to take with me; no time spent idle waiting for something or someone; no commuting to work. All travel is more efficient; I move only from destination to destination without intervening trips to a stationary home.

Far from having a primitive way of life, I enjoy electric lights, running hot and cold water, shower, gas range and heater. And all are "self-contained" – not dependent on external utility connections. With occasional refills of water, gasoline, and propane, I can enjoy my "modern conveniences" anywhere a rugged truck will take me.

At first I was crowded; especially when my rolling voluntary society doubled in population. But after consigning seldom-used items to storage, adding under-chassis compartments, and carefully rearranging, the interior is neat, belongings are accessible and space is adequate for two people.

Like many other self-liberating activities, mobile living is safest in the largest city or wildest wilderness. Cops have bothered me only twice in four months of living aboard; both times were in farming areas where, while traveling, I had stopped on (unposted) private land;

patrolling deputies asked me to move on. I have no problems parking on city streets at night, usually in apartment residential areas. On jobs I often stay in the company parking lot. Only rarely have I rented space – the backyards of friends – when doing work which immobilizes the truck for several days.

This way of life is very economical. My almost-new housecar, including much gear I have added, has cost under $6000 – a fraction of the price of a comparable yacht or a well-equipped retreat home, not to mention a cracker-box in the suburbs. And living expenses for two total about $120 per month, including $55 for food, $20 for gasoline, $10 for maintenance, $10 rental for storage space, and $25 for miscellaneous.

So far I have been too busy to travel extensively or to seek out especially attractive campsites. But already I have lived many exquisite days and evenings at beaches, mountains and forests. I am still learning the way of a modern nomad, but already I am free.

(from INNOVATOR, March 1968)

(Editor's Note: See the Introduction to adjust the prices mentioned above for inflation.)

Choosing a Van for Living Aboard

During the past five years two of us have lived in a motor vehicle three-quarters of the time and in various tents one-quarter of the time. The following are based on our experience and that of personal acquaintances.

Don't expect high vonu in a van. Have "acceptable" ID. A four-wheeled vehicle needs/makes trails and so is difficult to hide well. We have really tried, yet even in our most secluded squat spots, we get hassled (asked impertinent questions) once every couple of years or so. Nevertheless a camper or van may be ideal for someone in transition out of that society – ours has served us well this way.

Don't plan to travel much unless you have plenty of money. Don't buy a cheap well-worn van to move across the continent in unless you are already a fairly-skilled mechanic. Overall costs per mile of a "one-ton" vehicle will be about double those of a small imported automobile.

Single-piece vehicles (vans and motorhomes) and pickup campers both have their advantages. A van is lighter, sturdier has a lower center of gravity and is less wind resistant. Campers are mass produced and often cost less for the same comforts, may be more flexible, and cheaper to license in some states.

Buy instead of build, unless you are already experienced. The money you save building your own camper or making major changes in a van will be a very low return on your time. The experience gained is not very useful except for building more campers. If you do build, don't expect to achieve the overall quality of a factory-built until your *second* one.

Have at least a one-ton vehicle (at least 9000 lbs GVW); maybe one-and-one-half or two-ton. But check out the idiosyncrasies of the extorters in the states you expect to license and drive in. In many states vehicles over one-ton rating are supposed to stop at weigh stations and have commercial plates.

Have plenty of traction and a very low-speed bottom gear for getting off the road. Four-wheel drive is often desireable though expensive; next best is dual-rear wheels with most of the weight on them. VW microbuses and most three-speed standard transmission vehicles don't have a low enough low gear.

Avoid vehicles much longer than a big car – 20 feet – and trailers if you will go into cities or off the road much. Two small vans are more expensive than one big bus, but handier. Also beware of campers with long low overhang.

Furnishings recommended for living aboard most of the time: good insulation; furnace with exhaust vented to outside (I like a propane floor furnace with pilot for quickness of heat, simplicity and no smoke; a very small and light wood stove would be nice for backup); good ventilation; screens on all openings; cooking stove, probably propane, at least two burners; sink draining to waste-water can which can be removed for emptying; five gallon water with spigot which can be set over sink for use, taken down for filling and when moving; propane lamp (or possibly Alladin kerosene lamp) for main light with 12 volt bulbs for quick light and backup; dual batteries; dual propane tanks; polyurethane foam pad for mattress – light, fairly cheap, doesn't mildew; black-out shades or drapes over all windows; plenty of cabinets, closets, drawers and work surfaces. Ideally most bulky furnishings – cabinets, sinks, tables, etc. – are firmly mounted yet easily removed for use of vehicle for hauling – this I haven't seen in factory builts.

Furnishings not recommended: any appliances such as refrigerator or air conditioner which use 120 volt electricity in quantities too large to be supplied by an inverter; john hard-mounted on the vehicle (if a flush toilet is wanted, get Portapotti or a similar make which is a portable self-contained unit and can be removed for emptying); vehicle-mounted water system (we have one but leave it drained much of the year so we don't have to worry about freeze-up); shower and hot-water heater (again, we have one but find we'd usually rather jump in a creek, even in January, or take a sponge bath than spend a half-hour removing impedimentia from the shower, filling the tank, turning on the heater, etc.); unvented heater (fumes are harmful).

Minimize windows in a van if it will be in a city much. I'd consider a skylight (but not a bubble top unless it was somehow retractable).

Squatting and permission-parking both have their advantages and drawbacks. If squatting, one pays no rent. And one has a greater choice of spots including more secluded locations and so is less frequently hassled. Parking with permission, one spends less time finding spots, and is less likely to have to move when hassled – which can be important if one is in the middle of a major overhaul. Permission parking doesn't offer greater security – bludg insist on access to all trails and bludg usually first ask for ID. "We have permission to park here; you can check with our landlord" isn't a sufficient answer. Squatting for up to two weeks – sometimes longer – is legal on all land not otherwise posted. Chances of being prosecuted for trespassing are practically zero so long as there is no littering, open fires or vandalism; few land-owners wish to provoke people – too easy to set grudge fires. After several years experience we find we squat about 80% of the time; permission park about 20% of the time.

(from VONU LIFE 73, March 1973, page 37)

Further Report on Shelter

Dr. Gatherer and I are living in an A-tent made by placing polyethylene film (20 feet wide) over a rope strung between two trees. Our tent is 9 feet wide, 7 to 8 feet high in the middle, and 35 feet long! This is the first time we have had ample vonu work space sheltered from the rain and snow. One change we have made from our previous A-tents is to leave the ends open, which results in less underside condensation – no drips. We plan to fabricate triangular sections from scavenged cloth which will cover the ends (under the poly) to stop breezes and allow some solar heating. Another change: bracing poles (two pairs) are also placed in an A shape which leaves an unencumbered walkway down the middle. Cost of the poly plus rope was about $15.

Near one end of the A-tent lays our newest creation, in which I lie typing this: we call it a foam hut. It's about 9 feet long by 4 feet wide and 2 feet high, tapering toward the foot end. It is made of 2-inch polyurethane foam, glued together with a special cement (which may be 3M77, the can which was purchased at Hill's in Grant's Pass, is unlabeled). In one side of the hut is the door, covered by a flap of one-inch foam to which rocks are tied at the bottom to keep it snug. In the other side is a window, covered inside and out with a transparent vinyl-type plastic. (The foam itself would probably pass enough light now, but foam darkens with age.) In the roof at the head end is a screened hole for extra ventilation when our kerosene lamp is lit or in warm weather; a piece of foam plugs the hole when not needed. The foam alone (open cell) provides sufficient ventilation for breathing.

The hut is sort of like a giant sleeping bag except that the domed roof is firm enough to hold position. Under the floor, extending from shoulders to knees when sleeping, is an extra 3 by 4 ½ foot piece of 2 inch foam for comfort and additional insulation.

Based on the few temperature readings so far, the hut provides about 20°F above outside temperature with one person inside, 35° two. This is the body heat alone; when the lamp is burning we must open the door. The coldest morning so far: outside temperature was 20°, inside 57°. We were comfortable nude under 3 blankets.

The foam hut is a big step forward for us in comfort-with-vonu. Until now, when tent camping in winter, we could be comfortable huddled in a sleeping bag doing nothing but reading, on one hand; or doing strenuous physical work, on the other. But how does one typewrite, sew, or repair machinery – work requiring bare hands – in below freezing temperatures? Keeping a stove going for heat means much extra work and less vonu. Incidentally, this issue of VL is the first one typed and pasted up in a tent; until now we have done it in our van.

The foam hut is also a boon for Dr. Gatherer's sprout farm – a tray of glass jars keeping warm with me in the head end. Sprouts grow poorly or not at all during cold weather if just in a tent.

The hut weights about 20 pounds and rolls up into a bulky but backpackable bundle. So far it survived, undamaged, one trip from our van to our base camp. About four 45" by 76" sheets of 2 inch foam went into the construction. Material cost about $50; fabrication (not counting design time) took two days and required two people at times.

We expect to live in our tent and hut full-time this winter except for our brief trip in our van to the Bay area. Our van is presently stashed several miles away; we are still using it for work requiring electricity, which we don't have at camp yet. In the future we expect to use our van mainly for 'import-export' transportation.

(from VONU LIFE 4, November 1971)

40 By 8 Feet of Shelter for $30 and One Day

Tents I've seen for sale are ill-suited for full-time living in wet, forested areas such as the Pacific Northwest. They are dark and dank inside, and unnecessarily expensive for the space they provide.

Two years ago we were living in a tipi-shaped military surplus tent. After two days of steady rain, condensation or leaks (we weren't sure which) dripped from every irregularity and soaked us and our gear. In disgust we moved out, tied a rope between two trees, threw a piece of plastic over it, and found this was a big improvement. There was still condensation, but it ran down the plastic instead of dripping on us. The plastic passed plenty of light and was inexpensive. Since then we've experimented with several variations, all using polyethylene film ("builder's plastic").

Based on experience so far, here is how I would erect a base-camp shelter for two in a heavily forested spot, where there is little wind or direct sunlight, and where winters are mild enough to live without artificial heat — temperatures seldom below 20°.

I buy a fifty-foot roll of clear 6-mil polyethylene, 20 feet wide. This costs about $15 and weighs about 30 pounds. This will make a tent that is 35 to 40 feet long, 8 feet wide at the ground and 6 to 7 feet high in the center. This size is not excessive for a camp which two will occupy for several months; there are not the shelves and cabinets of a cabin or camper — much ground area is used for storage. Polyethylene in wide widths is sold by Sears, Wards and many building-supply stores. I also buy a hundred feet of inexpensive polypropylene rope (at least 1000 pound test) and several hundred feet of lighter cord — cost about $6. Polypropylene doesn't rot as do natural fibers, and stretches less than nylon.

I probably spend several days scouting a good site. I look for a 10-by-40 foot strip which needs little clearing but is among evergreen trees and high brush for shade and privacy. The strip may bend or zigzag, it need not be straight. If possible I avoid spots which show signs of washing during heavy rains. (See figure 1.)

When clearing I cut as little as possible. Along the edge I tie back branches instead of cutting. I may ditch around the high side for drainage. I check for dead trees or large branches which might blow down in a storm and pull or cut them down.

(Transcriber's Note: Figures 1-4 are below.)

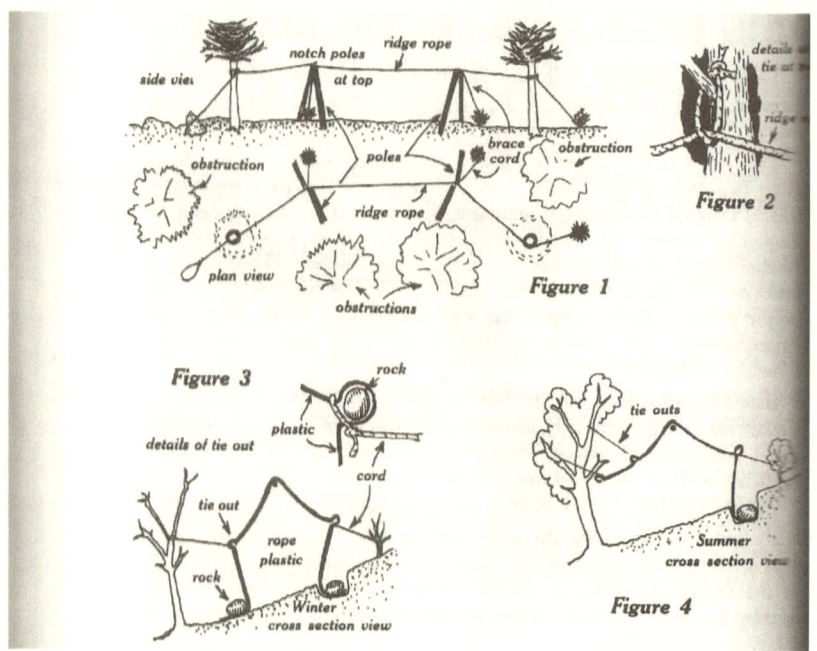

Figure 1

Figure 2

Figure 3

Figure 4

I string the rope between two trees at the ends of the strip. If the trees are small I brace to large boulders or the bases of bushes. I do not tie around a small tree; instead I tie the ridge rope up to a branch. (See figure 2.) This is to avoid damaging bark. If there is not a conveniently located tree at one end of the strip, I cut a post from a dead tree and brace it erect. If I am angling the shelter around obstructions (as shown in figure 1), I cut poles and brace them in pairs where the ridge rope changes direction. This also minimizes sag of the ridge rope.

I drape the polyethylene over the ridge rope, between the end trees. During winter I tie both sides outward a couple of feet from the ground, then angle inward at the bottom and anchor with rocks, logs or dirt. (See figure 3.) This shape allows the snow to slide off the tent. (If the tent were delta-shaped, the snow would pile up on the sides and stretch the plastic.) I tie to the plastic every few feet by bunching it over a small pebble ½ inch to ¾ inch diameter; no cutting is necessary.

If I use a ground plastic, I leave a few inches of bare ground between its edges and the sides of the tent, so that condensation does not run onto the ground plastic. For the same reason I do not place objects in contact with the tent. If I do not ditch, in winter I keep possessions which could be damaged by water off the ground – even in a well-drained spot water will run in once the ground outside becomes saturated.

In warm weather I remove the anchor rocks along one side and tie the plastic out for greater ventilation. I leave the other side anchored to block wind. (See figure 4.)

The poly tent provides shelter only from rain, snow, dew and wind. I can keep out insects by adding large pieces of curtain material or netting to the ends and open side. But more likely I only protect the bed area by rigging a mosquito bar over it. (Herters sells one of nylon, 76 x 36 x 36 inches for about $6.) During fall and winter when days are short and we use artificial light in the evenings, I rig a blackout tarp over the bed – a 12 by 16 foot piece of black polyethylene suffices.

If we cook within the tent, we use a small propane stove. If we cook on a wood stove, we do so away from the tent under a fly (all sides open) of black poly.

This design isn't suitable for a sunny location. Sunlight deteriorates ordinary clear polyethylene in six months (I've read). Other problems: the tent becomes very warm; the plastic casts reflections visible for hundreds of yards. Monsanto 602 or some other plastic made especially for greenhouse use will withstand sunlight for two years (it is claimed). One source is A.M. Leonard and Sons, Box 316, Piqua, Ohio 45356. 602 costs about twice as much as polyethylene.

Comparing this shape with the covered-wagon-shaped polyethylene dwelling described in The Mother Earth News #16: The covered-wagon-shape provides more standup space for the same amount of plastic, but involves more work, uses more trees, doesn't shed snow, and is likely to have condensation drips.

This tent has proven satisfactory in the Sikiyous from about April through October, tolerable in winter with the addition of a foam hut. And it is bright, roomy, simple and inexpensive.

(from VONULIFE 1973, March 1973, page 13)

Foods for Storage: Some Preliminary Suggestions

Our food objective is to continue eating without being vulnerable. "Living off the land" sounds appealing. But doing it successfully month after month in all seasons, requires much experience and long hours. After about two years of vonu living, Dr. Gatherer and I obtain perhaps 20% of our food on the average from hunting and foraging; this is figuring raw weights – in calories foraged food provides less than 5%. We expect to do better as we gain experience and have more time – at present various forms of shelter are still taking most of our time. But a new vonuan should not expect to live off the land immediately.

Conventional agriculture is of course hopelessly vulnerable. We have thought about cryptoculture – growing crops in small, irregular concealed plots. But there are many problems to be solved. It's feasible right now maybe for high-value crops such as pot, but not for the bulk of one's food. So the way to become as vonu as possible as quickly as possible is to eat mostly storable foods. These must be "imported" of course, but not every day or even month – many will store 10 years or longer. And in 10 year's time, we can most likely learn to live off the land if we have to.

We seek foods which are storable for a year or longer, preferably at ordinary temperatures; inexpensive – total cost not much over $100 per person per year; nourishing – a healthful diet without large additions of fresh foods; light and compact; tasty; easily tested for edibility.

food	gr/day	calories	protein	fat	lb/yr	¢/lb	$/yr	storage min	max
wheat, whole grain	188	640	24	2.9	150	6	9.00	400	750
brown rice	94	333	7	1.5	75	12	9.00	75	150
popcorn	38	97	5	1.7	30	13	3.90	30	60
lentils	75	255	15	1.0	60	15	9.00	100	200
red beans	25	85	7	0.2	20	17	3.40	50	100
dry non-fat milk	25	90	9		20	35	7.00	25	50
dry (dead) yeast	6	16	2		5	70	3.50	5	10
nuts (hulled weight)	95	570	17	52.0	75	40	30.00	75	150
dry fruit	31	83			25	40	10.00	25	50
honey	87	256			70	20	14.00	360	720
totals	*664*	*2425*	*86*	*59.3*	*530*		*103.80*		*2240*

Here are the storable foods we are presently eating, and/or expect to eat in quantity over the next year.

All of the above figures are per person. Protein and fat are grams per day; storage is in pounds. We may substitute some other grains and pulses for some of the brown rice or lentils, etc., but this will give an idea.

Weights, cost and calories assume one is sedentary (or small) and living exclusively on stores. Of course we need many more calories when active. But we eat other foods; not only wild foragings but some purchased fresh foods during trips "outside." The total cost includes $5 allowance for food supplements. The maximum and minimum storage are objectives for this autumn; we hope to eventually increase these to a ten year supply as we gain knowhow and facilities.

Comparing nutritional elements with those recommended:

substance	recommended min.	provided by above	supplements used
protein	70 gr/day	86 gr/day	none
fat	54 gr/day	59 gr/day	none
calcium	0.8 to 4 gr/day	0.6 gr/day	2.0 gr/day
phosphorus		2.0 gr/day	none
iron	10 mg/day	21.7 mg/day	none
Vit. A	5000 units/day	586 units/day	5000 units/day
Vit B1	1.6 mg/day	2.8 mg/day	none
Vit. B2	1.8 mg/day	2.1 mg/day	none
niacin	21 mg/day	21.9 mg/day	none
Vit. C	75 mg/day	negligible	200 mg/day
Vit. D	400 units/day	none	sunshine or 400 u/day
Vit. E	25 units/day ?	substantial	200 units/day

Apparently not much is known about the amount of fat needed, except that some polyunsaturated fatty acids are considered essential. The conventional wisdom right now seems to be that 20% of calories should come from fat with at least two-thirds of that from unsaturated. However, many people, especially in oriental countries, live healthfully with 10% or less of total calories from fat. I have eaten as little as 6% for a month or more but developed a craving for fat. Since fat foods are the most expensive, the most difficult to store and are often contaminated, this deserves further investigation.

At the moment we are avoiding processed oils and margarine entirely. Not only are the ingredients apt to be of low quality but various chemicals of unknown toxicity are introduced during commercial processing. And such oils can apparently become appreciably rancid without change in taste; rancid oils are reputed to be a major cause of aging. Oil sold by health food stores, to which no antioxidants are added, can be even more dangerous unless it has been continuously refrigerated since manufacture; the oil becomes rancid quicker. The information on oil rancidity is scanty and often contradictory; in the absence of more knowledge we are playing it safe.

Nuts we eat include walnuts, filberts, almonds, peanuts, and/or sunflower seeds; which ones we purchase depends on price and taste preferences. The above weights are for hulled nuts; however all but the sunflower seeds are purchased and stored unhulled. Raw sunflower seeds are purchased (hopefully) shortly after the hulling and placed immediately in a CO_2 atmosphere. In the future we hope to store all nuts, especially sunflower seeds, at not over 35°F; however, we have stored nuts for a year at 55°F with no appreciable change in taste. Hulled sunflower seeds sprout well; a test of their condition – how good a test for oil rancidity we don't know. In the past we have used soy beans as a fat source. But soy beans are apparently even more difficult to store than nuts. Ominously, soy beans will not sprout if stored at room temperature for more than one year.

Our present diet includes moderate amounts of powdered milk and dry food yeast. These foods are questionable nutritionally: their processing and storage as fine particles forms oxidized substances which are apparently a major cause of degenerative diseases.[1] Milk is controversial in other ways as well: some nutritionists recommend plenty of it, *especially* non-fat dry milk; others do not recommend it unless it is raw milk fresh from the cow – drunk within a few minutes of milking; still others are down on milk in all forms – these people include not only vegetarians but some who recommend fresh meat. Also milk and yeast are relatively expensive and difficult to store. And they are not needed for protein content. But, with the present primitive state of the 'science' of nutrition, I prefer to hedge my bet by including at least some foods of animal origin. And I seem to digest milk well; easier than wheat or beans. As we grow in ability to hunt and trap I intend to phase out milk.[2] We have stored dry milk (Challenge non-instant, Jorgensen X-grade) for a year at 55°F average with no change in taste.

Dried meat and fish are much too expensive to be considered. And we can get small amounts of meat without even spending time hunting by killing the slow animals we meet: an occasional rattlesnake, crayfish or porcupine. Anyone avoiding animal foods entirely should include a Vitamin B12 supplement; B12 does not occur in vegetables.

Wheat continues to form a large part of our diet and an even larger part of our stores, even though it is not as palatable or digestible as rice and many other grains. Not only is it inexpensive – it stores well. And samples can be sprouted to test condition. Rice sprouts poorly if at all and is reputedly difficult to store – oil becomes rancid. Unless rice can be stored at a low temperature, white rice may be better than brown, despite the loss of B vitamins and the flat taste. Lentils and red beans both sprout well; we know of no special storage problems. We eat more lentils because we like the taste better.

We purchase only whole grain; never flour or cracked cereals. Commercial flour and the pastries made from it are apparently the major cause of arteriosclerosis, arthritis and similar degenerative diseases.[1] Whole wheat flour and whole grain cereals such as oatmeal and granola may be even more harmful than white flour because the oils quickly become rancid after grinding due to oxidation of vitamin E, the anti-oxidant; the vitamin E is oxidized within days after grinding.

Dry fruit may not be justified for nutritional content but is included for taste variety and related psychological reasons; we don't want to unconsciously associate "goodies" with *that* society. For price reasons the fruit is mostly raisins, figs, dates and prunes. We eat dry fruits mostly during winter and spring; during summer and autumn we forage fresh berries. We have experimentally dried several kinds of berries with good results but not yet in sufficient quantities to replace imports. Honey is also not justified nutritionally, but a generous amount is included, not only because it stores indefinitely, but to avoid any craving for sweets. White granulated sugar is suspect as a food; in experimental animal feedings refined sugar produced ailments in cases where equivalent amounts of honey or other sweets did not.

No dehydrated vegetables are included. In this area at least a few greens can be foraged the year around at lower altitudes. These and sprouted alfalfa seed, lentils and wheat provide taste variety and a nutritional safety factor.

For a calcium supplement we are using bone meal, but it may switch to oyster shell if we can purchase it in powdered form. Oyster shell tastes better than bone meal and has a higher calcium to phosphorous ratio. Some prefer dolomite because it has magnesium as well as calcium. Some nutritionists say the minimum calcium required is 0.8 grams per day; others say twice as much calcium as phosphorous which for us would be 4 grams per day. This is further complicated by the relative assimilation of Ca and Ph from various foods.

Other supplements presently include alfalfa seeds for sprouting, vitamins A, C and E, kelp for trace minerals, and various seasonings. Vitamins C and dry E will apparently store indefinitely in sealed, opaque containers; vitamin A and oil E must be kept cool. Vitamin E reputedly counteracts the effects of rancid oil in the body so we take a substantial dose in addition to what our food supplies.

Dr. Gatherer and I differ on the relative merits of organic and non-organic food. Our present policy (compromise) is to pay a substantial premium for organically grown fruits and fresh vegetables (when we buy them) but no more than 10% premium on grain or nuts.

Our long-term storage of grains and nuts is within an inert atmosphere in polyethylene bags in sealed drums. To obtain the inert atmosphere we put ½ ounce dry ice per gallon volume in bottom of drum, pour in food, tie bag loosely and place top loosely on drum. After a few hours the dry ice will evaporate (bottom of drum will no longer feel cold) and pressure will be equalized. Then we tie the bag and seal the drum tightly. We have stored wheat this way for over three years (and it was at least a year old when we bought it); it still sprouts well.

The yearly cost can be reduced to $60 or less per year by increasing consumption of wheat and reducing consumption of everything else. But while such a diet still provides adequate protein, B vitamins, etc., we hesitate to depend heavily on a single food, both because of nutritional uncertainty and for psychological reasons.

[1] "Stale Food Versus Fresh Food," Robert S. Ford, Magnolia Laboratories, 701 Beach Blvd., Pascagoula, MS 39567. "When food is stored too long, particularly after it has been ground up, cooked or exposed to air, sunlight and microbes, portions of the cholesterol and other waxes, fats, oils, proteins, etc., become oxidized, hardened, dried up and changed into durable non-food materials which the cells of our bodies cannot utilize. When we eat these stale foods, some of the deteriorated materials become semi-permanently lodged in our flesh as

arteriosclerotic deposits... The condition that makes fatty rubbish from flour so much more dangerous than any other food is its finely ground form, so fine that it can slip through the walls of our intestines with the food stream and get into our blood very easily, whereas if it were coarser most of it would pass out of the body with little harm... Taking both the food and the quantity usually eaten into consideration, flour products such as bread, biscuits, and ready-to-eat cereals, cake and crackers are the big killers, probably accounting for 60% of arteriosclerosis damage. Next come bacon, ham, sausages, sardines, etc., accounting for perhaps 20%. Mayonnaise, cheese, margarine and ice cream probably cause less than 15% of the problem, and the other miscellaneous items are only a trifle." Ford recommends eating as many foods raw as possible, and cooking only by steaming or boiling.

I've always been rather skeptical of most health-food advocates because their explanations tend to be mystical and their recommendations contradictory. But I'm quite impressed by Ford's work, partly because his hypothesis integrates a lot of seemingly-contradictory evidence. I recommend his booklet despite its price: $3.50 for 48 pages – money back guarantee, however.

[2] Many adults, including most American Indians and Blacks, lack an enzyme needed for converting milk sugar, and are given indigestion by milk.

(from VONU LIFE #3, September 1971)

(Editor's Note: To roughly adjust these prices for inflation, see the Introduction.)

Soybeans

Thanks to Johnny Reb for the tip that many soybeans fail to sprout because they are hybrids and therefore sterile, not because of deterioration. Whether or not one wishes to eat sprouts, it's nice to be able to sprout as a test of condition. As previously mentioned, soybeans which came (according to the man who sold them) from Arrowhead Mills (Box 866, Hereford, TX 79045; $5/50 pounds fob) have sprouted well and taste delicious that way after a short steaming. Unsprouted, these don't taste much different than soybeans we bought over two years ago which never have sprouted well.

(from VONU LIFE #6, March 1972)

(Editor's Note: Soybeans that sprout well have a black spot on them, like black eyed peas. Non-sprouting soybeans lack this spot. I am now (early 1983) paying $12.00 for 50 pounds of soybeans (wholesale price) from a local food co-op.)

Opting Out – Vonu Economic Strategies

We encounter vonuists who are succeeding, also some who aren't. A few of the latter may be drifters or dilettantes. But most are sincere, capable strivers who fail, not for lack of ability or hard work, but through errors of strategy.

Some of these errors delayed Rayo's own vonu. The following suggestions apply mainly to wilderness ways of vonu under present conditions. Of course they are generalities – there are exceptions. You probably already "know" most of these – i.e., consciously agree with them. But they may be useful as a check of your subconscious values which show up in performance. Values often lag conscious conclusions.

Be as vonu as you can. Vonu is not an all-or-nothing thing. There is no way to be **completely** invulnerable to coercion. But this doesn't justify giving up and "adjusting" to depredation, any more than lack of complete invulnerability to disease justifies neglecting health. Select approaches which yield maximum vonu per time and resources expended.

Vonu your home first. "Domestic" activities – sleeping, eating, cleaning, grooming, mending, reading, writing, listening to music, lovemaking, meditating, exercising, conversing, child care, etc. – comprise most of one's life. A vonu home seems essential for psychological wellbeing. And domestic activities are relatively easy to vonu; they do not require elaborate equipment or deep involvement with outsiders.

In contrast, earning money takes up only a relatively small part of one's life. At $2 per hour clear, 300 hours of city labor – one month with overtime – will pay for eight months of vonu living. And earning money usually requires export – difficult to accomplish without interference. So vonu should begin at home.

Most non-vonu homes and even entire cities are only "bedroom" communities; residents do not earn their money there. Most new towns begin this way. While it is nice for a vonu home to be financially productive, this isn't essential.

Have savings before moving. During your first year or two in a wilderness or other vonu environment, expect to be occupied developing shelter and learning vonu-living skills. You will have little time for money earning even if opportunities are at hand. Suggested minimum savings for prospective tent dwellers: $2000 for one person, $1200 each additional person in family. These amounts include: initial equipment costs of $800 for one person, $400 for each additional person; per year expenses for two years of $600 for one person, $400 for each additional person.

$600 or $400 per year assumes: mostly staple foods; no rent except for maybe a storage garage; little driving; relatively few luxuries, food fetishes or status games. Some vonuans live on much less, but don't count on doing so during your first two years. Our total expenses (of two people, for two years ending autumn 1971) averaged $622 per year per person, including substantial equipment costs and business expenses, which, unfortunately, we didn't record separately. We lived about 7 months in tents, the rest of the time in the van. Van was bought before record period.

Earn money by exporting labor at first. Don't expect to earn money immediately gathering herbs or dredging gold if you have time left from home development. What opportunities are there may be for wilderness income require considerable skills to pay off. Scrounging for jobs in a small town is a bad scene. Get jobs in cities (if that is what you have done); preferably temporary employment which fits your living patterns. If you have a freemate or children, let them remain at your vonu home while you "commute" weekly or seasonally. Why subject them to bludg, smog and chance of nuclear incineration?

Don't change vocations until you achieve a vonu home. If you can clear $2 or more per hour in your present (non-vonu) job, you will probably achieve vonu quickest by staying with it until you have enough capital to cut loose for two years. Don't spend time getting into a slightly better non-vonu occupation still dependent on that society if you expect to live most of your life out of that society. A do-at-home vocation such as freelance writing or mail-order selling is best developed after you have a vonu home.

Be wary of get-rich-easy schemes. "If he's so smart, why ain't he already rich? If he is rich, why does he want my pocket change?" Not all such schemes are conscious swindles; many a promoter sincerely believes he has found a unique way to financial independence. But, unless he is already affluent, you don't know that it worked. Even if it worked for him it may not for you – opportunities change. But even if you could make it work, it probably requires heavy psycho-investment/involvement with the coerced economy; more than would a work-a-day job.

Live frugally while in the coerced economy. It saddens us to meet would-be vonuans who, after working ten years at a well-paying job, don't have savings enough to opt out for even six months. Tactics for saving: Make a "crash" program of it – save a high proportion of income for a short time. Take savings off the top – a certain percentage of income – and live on what is left. Concentrate on big or continuing expenses – usually shelter, transportation and food, but also be careful that "small luxuries" don't get big. Double up with others to save rent. Drive little. See "Foods for Storage – Some Preliminary Suggestions" for food economy tips.

Make part of your monetary savings untouchable until required capital is accumulated. Don't rationalize that such-and-such item is really preparation for vonu (unless you already have much experience in your intended life-style and know exactly what equipment and supplies you will need). Start outfitting at a local dump (discarded blankets, clothes, utensils), then try Salvation Army Stores, etc. You can gradually replace with better equipment after you are vonu, as you learn what you really need.

Keep money in simple, safe forms. If your savings are small and short-term (under $2000, under two years) the best form for North Americans (all factors considered including ease of conversion) is probably U.S. or Canadian $20 bills well-hidden in several places. Currency will suffer inflation losses but, for small amounts, any other form is apt to be more trouble than it is worth.

For a larger amount or a longer time, investigate gold and silver (bars, or coins priced at close to metal value only), Swiss banks, etc. Avoid savings bonds or savings accounts in U.S. institutions. Don't speculate in stocks, real-estate, commodities, rare coins, etc. (unless you are already a full-time professional at one of these).

Seek vonu, not self-sufficiency per se. A few vonuans cannot live in complete, permanent isolation without many years, perhaps generations of learning. And "primitivism," even if achieved, would result in increasing vulnerability as aggressor's technology and methods change.

A vonu association of a few dozen to a few hundred will likely be only a little more self-sufficient than one family. A remote (non-vonu) town of this size probably has a welder, dairy, nurse – maybe even a small machine shop. But most goods and many services are more economical to import than to produce there. Even in a country of 100,000 people, such as Bahama, most items are imported. The major advantage of a vonu association compared to a lone family: easier/better import-export.

Some people talk of developing a "parallel economy" producing all essential supplies and spare parts, before concerning themselves much with physical invulnerability. But this supposes involvement of millions of people. And what would a non-vonu alternate economy be, anyway? An enterprise vulnerable to the State must operate under State rules. This, not the rhetoric of its founders, will determine the way it operates, assuming it is a "success." Function determines form. A real alternate economy requires vonu (though not necessarily wilderness forms exclusively).

A vonuan can minimize dependence upon the coerced economy by stockpiling essentials. But he cannot achieve complete invulnerability. Again, vonu is not an all-or-nothing thing.

Select companions who are doing. If you link up with others, be it a single freemate or a number of associates, look for people who are already living in large part as they want to live. Of course a life-style isn't static – a couple may go further into vonu than would a single person. But this should be evolutionary growth from present living patterns, not a quantum jump. (Quantum jumps are often desireable but are best attempted alone.)

Many a man will say, and sincerely believe, that he wants to vonu just as soon as he finds "the right woman" or "the right group" to do it with, but he doesn't want to do it alone. However, how do you (and he) know that he can do it, until he does it for a substantial time? If he can't stand living alone – if he soon gets bored with himself – chances are he will soon get bored with you, too. So suggest that he do it alone for a year or so before trying to link up.

Long unspectacular living in relative isolation is more significant than an occasional Great Adventure such as sailing a yacht around Cape Horn or scaling 25,000-foot Mt. Fuchiguchi. Some (not all) Great Adventurers are unable to stimulate themselves and structure their own time – get bored easily. Also be skeptical of the guy who says he "has done it all," but is living conventionally. Why did he quit?

An important exception: There are presently more male than female vonuans (though the ratio is not as large as talk would indicate;

relatively fewer girls are bullshitters). So if you are a woman, you can be a buyer in a buyer's market. You can quickly achieve vonu, even though you lack the capital and experience, by finding a man with these. In this case, it's especially important that your prospective freemate offer proven capability, not just dreams and schemes.

Don't feel that you should provide half the capital or income; you offer your own values and talents (and not just erotic ones). By analogy, silver has no more uses than aluminum, but it has different ones and it is scarcer, so it doesn't exchange for aluminum one-for-one. Why should you? Most women adapt easier to vonu living than do most men, perhaps because they are more self-sufficient psychologically; their self-esteem depends more on personal and home activities, less upon a "career" involved with that society.

Stay relatively mobile so you can respond to emerging opportunities or link up with others. Own only what you can move easily or abandon without regret. Avoid large, elaborate dens, at least for the first few years. We can move our base camp and all equipment (except long-term supply caches) in six weeks, which includes three weeks for exploration and preparation of a new site plus three weeks for transport of up to 1000 pounds – by backpack to roadhead, by truck to new roadhead, by backpack to new site.

- *Second thoughts:* Reading this, I'm not entirely satisfied with my treatment of export, especially the second, fourth and fifth topics. Regardless of proportion of time spent, some will value vonu in export more than vonu at home. So let's concentrate on what we value most – succeed at our own thing – and trade; then we'll always have more vonu everywhere.

(from VONU LIFE #5, January 1972)

(Editor's Note: To adjust these dollar amounts for inflation, see the Introduction.)

On Acquisition of "Private" Land

While I often squat on "public lands," I have found "private property" useful in some situations; especially for unattended parking of a four-wheel vehicle and for storage of other things too big and/or not valuable enough to hide really well. I make these suggestions:

Don't try to substitute "legal" ownership for physical invulnerability. Land you "own" is not truly yours. The State will try to tell you what you can or can't do with it, and will tax you for the privilege. Depending on local regulations, you may not be able to legally build a shack, put in a septic tank, plant trees, cut trees, shoot game, or grow crops without special permission from various bludg agencies. "Your" land may be "condemned" and taken away from you for a freeway, a dam site, or a "wilderness area." "Ownership" does not even constitute a bonafide lease from the State since the State can unilaterally change its terms at any time.

Lease instead of buy if your expected use is short-term (a few years or less). And preferably lease from a sympathetic landlord. This can save a lot of hassles.

Count the purchase price as an expense, not an investment. Taxes on visible property are the only taxes easily collected, and will tend to rise to the rental value of the property, wiping out "equity." (Income and sales taxes are increasingly evaded and/or destroy their economic base.) Property taxes are already one-third or more of rental value in much of the U.S.; often in excess of rental value in NYC, resulting in abandonment of thousands of buildings. Of course some lands may increase in value in the short term. But land speculation, along with speculation in stocks, commodity futures, rare stamps, horse races and poker games, is rationally left to full-time professionals.

Lease or buy "waste" land to keep purchase price and taxes low. Avoid commercial farm land, commercial timber land, and land close to cities or recreational developments.

Obtain only a few acres, but close by a "national forest" or other large stretch of unowned ("government owned") land, as an access port (for foot nomads/trogs).

Get land with trees, brush and topography adequate to conceal anything you may leave on the surface from habitations, roads and the air. (Some counties are reportedly aerial mapping for tax assessment purposes.)

Purchase in name of someone ("real" or otherwise) who has few dealings in the servile society to minimize chances that the land will be confiscated as a result of lawsuit, unpaid income taxes, etc. The "owner" is preferably a woman – not subject to conscription, not expected to be employed. First check out the purchase procedure. Is I.D. required to purchase? To sell? Must purchaser appear anywhere in person?

Don't use land as a mailing address, nor as "legal home address" on driver's license or other I.D. Don't have a mailbox there. Don't have a telephone there. Maintain these addresses elsewhere. Caution everyone who uses land never to mention it as address. Bludg agencies cross-check each other's records more and more. Get on file with one and others will come asking why you are/aren't doing this and that.

Don't make permanent, visible installations or improvements. Limit surface structures to vans and trailers. Do not connect to commercial electricity or other utilities. If questioned as to land use, land is unoccupied, unimproved for occasional recreational use only. Hide vehicles as well as possible, also move occasionally.

Minimize use of access roads to minimize attention. "Commute" to town weekly or less often, preferably on the weekends when there is maximum "foreign" traffic and during darkness when vehicles are not easily identified.

Get land with heavy brush to discourage interlopers. "Build" extra bushes as necessary to encourage any hikers to go around rather than through your important places. Artificial barriers – more elaborate than a chain across the driveway – are seldom worthwhile. A high electrified fence may keep out an occasional hunter but will arouse curiosity as to what is going on. A well-concealed warning system will be of value if people live there often.

I have not discussed "conventional" aspects of land purchase, because I don't know them and because they will vary from place to place.

(from VONU LIFE #1, May 1971)

Vonu in Cities

Most discussions of vonu living assume unpopulated or far-away places. Concerning urban possibilities, five possible approaches come to mind.

The first and simplest is anonymity: Be visible but not noticeable. Conform outwardly while doing your own thing in secret. Be inconspicuous, as Allen Humble says in his article. But most of Humble's advice concerns what not to do. Where does Humble go to "do his own thing"? Probably not to his apartment. Renting under a *nom de plume* does not prevent inspection by landlord or police, or overhearing by nosy neighbors.

Humble speaks of children but I wonder if he has any. He says to keep children out of sight during school hours. I wouldn't want the job of keeping children quietly cooped up in an apartment during slave-school hours. Incidentally, I've heard that California has lowered slave age to six.

Regarding Humble's recommendation to avoid paying by check: I agree if the transaction is face-to-face, large or repeating. But selling small items by mail (like Vonu Life) for cash only isn't feasible, so you are welcome to pay by check. Urban anonymity offers no protection from such dangers as nuclear war. Despite these criticisms, I agree with most of Humble's recommendations, many of which apply to all vonuans, not just urban anonoymites.

I lived much of the way Humble advocates before taking up van nomadism. For me anonymity alone was unsatisfactory because of city psychological pressures. I was immersed in an alien culture with values hostile to my own. Whether or not I was especially vulnerable, I felt vulnerable.

I know of quite a few vonuists and libertarians who live Humble's way, but I know none who seem to like it for very long. Perhaps there are ways to cope with the psychological pressures. If you think you have found a way, tell us. But, personally, I prefer to live "far enough back in the woods..."

A way to reduce psychological pressures is to gather with fellows into a "ghetto" – a second approach to city vonu. One loses anonymity with respect to the larger culture as one develops subculture speech, customs, mannerisms and dress. But one becomes a relatively indistinguishable member of the subculture, requiring that any organized aggressor attack everyone or no one. "All (Chinese, Niggers, Hippies...) look alike." This doesn't always stop aggressors – witness Jews in Nazi Germany, Japanese in U.S.

The recommendations made by Walt Hayward presume ghettos of like-minded people. His objections against moving into the wildlands are directed to retreatists who hope to do it "at the last moment," not at vonuans who expect to live there most of the time.

Ghettos are also possible in rural areas. The Takilma area southeast of Cave Junction, Oregon, is almost a "freek" ghetto. While freeks may not be in the majority yet, there are enough to render the area unattractive for anti-freeks, causing most land up for sale to be bought by freeks, etc. – analogous to what happens in new Black ghettos in cities. How much protection this provides remains to be seen. There have been quite a few arrests for growing/using pot, etc. A bigger crunch will come when substantial numbers of freek children become old enough for slave school. (Will the "Supreme Court" require long-hairs and short-hairs to be intermixed by bussing? Or will it compel kids to cut their hair middle length, with the length set by the majority vote every four years?)

A third approach involves a blend of concealment and deception: construct hidden, sound-proofed apartments and workshops beneath or within an "owned" building ostensibly used for other purposes. Since such chambers could be blast, fire and fallout resistant, this approach offers some protection against nuclear attack as well as day-to-day predation. The family of Anne Frank (Diary of a Young Girl) tried (unsuccessfully) to hide this way during Nazi occupation of Holland. The hidden-chamber approach seems to have much potential; also many problems. I have not attempted it nor even thought much about it. I welcome the insights of anyone who has.

A fourth approach: Build a den or camouflaged camp on unowned land such as a "public park." This approach has much in common with wilderness vonu. Major advantage: easier access to city. Disadvantages: more difficult to conceal; general hazards of city including smog and nuclear threat. A man built a shack and lived undetected for 17 years in a Portland city park (reported in Preform-Inform). "Park squatting" might be done easiest by vonuans who first develop concealment skills in unpopulated remote areas, then opt for better city access.

The fifth approach: van nomadism with city squat-spots. Some differences from wilderness squatting: "Private" land, such as backyards of friends, is probably safer than streets for long stays. The vehicle need not be as self contained since utilities are close at hand. Off-the-road performance isn't important. Appearance, conventionality, license plates, etc., are important.

(from VONU LIFE #5, January 1972)

A Survey of Siskiyou Region

We don't wish to recognize states by saying "Southwestern-Oregon-and-Northern-California" so we say "Siskiyou Region." Siskiyou includes a wide variety of terrain, soil, climate and vegetation.

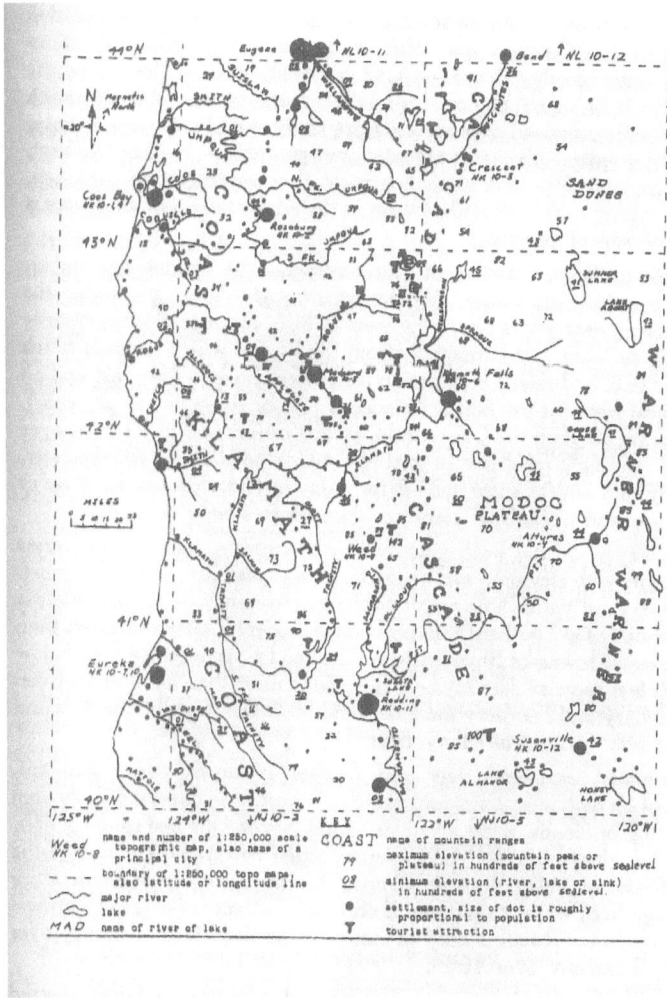

The Coast ranges are mostly sedimentary rocks – rather soft, easily eroded into soil. The Cascade and Warner ranges and the Modoc Plateau between are mostly volcanic – hard, not easily eroded. Their surface is bare rock in many places, especially in drier areas. The Klamath ranges are composed of many different kinds of rocks, from soft shales to hard granites. The rocks are often metamorphic – changed by heat, pressure and intrusions of molten rock, deep underground eons ago. Most mining in the region has been in the Klamath mountains; there is little mining at present.

Siskiyou Region has a hot, dry summer, June through September, and a mild, wet winter, November through April. In winter the prevailing west winds (from the west at high altitudes, not necessarily on the surface), bring moist air from the Pacific which deposits much snow, sleet and rain. Precipitation is heaviest close to the coast and on the west slope of the higher Cascades (80 or more inches per year), moderate between the Coast and the Cascade ranges (30 to 40 inches per year), and light most places east of the Cascades. In winter, typically, steady rain and/or snow will fall for a day or two; then several days of showers and occasional clearing; then more steady rain/snow.

In winter, on the west coast of North America, temperature varies primarily with elevation and secondarily with distance east of the coast. Temperature varies little with latitude (north-south) – some mountain communities in Southern California have colder (but dryer) winters than do coastal towns of Southeastern Alaska. In Siskiyou Region, below 2000 feet snow seldom lays on the ground more than a few days. Even January and February there are mild spells with highs in the 50's and 60's; also occasional sunny days.

Summer, especially July and August, is mostly sunny and hot, except on high mountains and along the coast. The coast is usually cool with fog or clouds, while 15 miles inland, beyond the first range of hills, the sun shines brightly. Blackberries ripen in two months earlier in the Rogue River Valley than on the coast. On the coast, mean temperature change from winter to summer is only 12° - September is the warmest month. In the Rogue Valley in summer, the daily high is usually over 90°, frequently over 100°.

On the Pacific Coast summer is somewhat warmer and dryer toward the south: July and August in central British Columbia are about like June and September in Siskiyou, and May and October in Southern California.

On the well-watered Coast ranges and western slopes of the Cascades, the commonest tree is douglas fir; on the east slope of the Cascades, the commonest tree is ponderosa pine; the plateau further east grows mostly brush. In the Klamath mountains vegetation depends very much on the soil; a lush forest may be growing on a pocket of decomposing shale while, a mile away, peridotite supports only stunted knobcone pine and manzanita bushes.

Little virgin timer remains, except where the trees are too small to be worth cutting; commercial forest is mostly second growth. Lumber remains the biggest industry of the region but is stable-to-declining.

Despite the mild climate there is relatively little agriculture. Not only is level land limited to a few river valleys, but the soil is leached in the winter and baked in summer. Even in the Rogue Valley, most crops need irrigation and fertilization. East of the Cascades there isn't the leaching problem but irrigation water is scarce. Even stock raising is not very extensive west of the Cascades; grasses are poor in minerals, hay and alfalfa are tucked in to supplement local forage.

During the last few years many non-vonuist agrarians, both freeks and retirees, have been attracted to Siskiyou because of its mild climate and proximity to major West Coast cities. This has bid up the price of what fair crop land there is. But now the net flow of these people seems to be away, to the Appalachians and Ozarks where land is less expensive and growing conditions relatively better.

What is bad for agrarians can be good for vonuans. Thousands of square miles are completely uninhabited except for berry bushes and herbs, deer and bear – and us. Except around a few settled areas and tourist attractions, one can walk a quarter mile away from a trail and be alone. Even in deer season, few people go far from the roads; the favorite hunting tactic of rednecks is to drive along, 2 or 3 in a pickup, and blast whatever they scare up. In many areas it is heavy brush; a formidable barrier to a stranger, but a friend of the vonuan who has worked out trails.

While there are few people in the back country, there are enough in the larger trading centers for comparative anonymity – everyone doesn't know everyone else. And these trading centers are close enough at hand so that transportation isn't a big problem. Furthermore, San Francisco, Los Angeles or Portland is only a day's drive away. For these reasons, vonu is easier for small groups to achieve in Siskiyou than in a more remote region, such as Yukon. And Siskiyou is the safest region in the U.S. in event of nuclear war; it is upwind and away from major targets.

So far we have explored very little of Siskiyou. Based on what we know now, the best sub-region for year-round vonuans is Klamath mountains with their great variety of terrain and vegetation including large areas of "wasteland," growing trees too small for timber, and brush. While Klamath mountains includes rugged 8000-foot peaks, there are also hundreds of valleys below snowline – desirable for someone who may be hunted as well as hunter. Water is no problem except on ridges – even small sub-tributary creeks flow the year round.

For summer van-nomads, Klamath mountains aren't too good; most terrain is too rugged or brushy to get a four-wheeled vehicle off of maintained trails. Lumbering (of douglas fir) is mostly by clear-cutting; unused trails soon grow over. The pine forests of the southern Cascades are better; at least this is true of areas we have seen between Medford and Klamath Falls; extensive areas are relatively level except for a few volcanic peaks; the forest is parklike with little brush. There are more tourists, however, and foraging seems not to be as good as in Coast and Klamath mountains. An Oregon city is better than a California city for local purchases and receiving mail; there is no sales tax in Oregon.

Maps Suggested

Forest Service Maps. These indicate land status ("public" or "private") and show most roads and jeep trails. Their road information is more up to date than are topographic maps. Scale of most of them is ½ inch equals one mile. There is no charge for these maps but, so far as we know, each must be individually ordered from (or picked up at) the headquarters of each National Forest.

In the list below, the numbers following each address indicate approximate range of latitude and longitude covered by the map. (To cover Klamath mountains, get Siskiyou, Six Rivers, Klamath and Rogue River maps.) Siskiyou National Forest, Box 440, Grants Pass, OR 97526, 41.8-43°N, 123.3-124.5°W, Rogue River National Forest, Box 520, Medford, OR 97501, 41.8-43°N, 122-123.2°W. Klamath National Forest, Yreka, CA (?), 41-42°N, 122.8-123.8°W. Shasta Trinity National Forest, Redding, CA 40-41.7°N, 120.8-123.5°W. (Ask for maps of Trinity and Shasta National Forests.) Modoc National Forests, Alturas, CA (?), 41-42°N, 120-122°W. Lassen National Forest, Susanville, CA

(?), 40-41°N, 120.5-122°W. Suislaw National Forest, Box 1148, Corvallis, OR 97330, 43.3-45°N, 123-124.5°W. Willamette National Forest, Box 1272, Eugene, OR 97401, 43.3-43.7°N, 121.8-122.5°W. Umpqua National Forest, Roseburg, OR, 42.8-44°N, 122-123°W. Deschutes National Forest, Bend, OR (?), 43-45°N, 121-122°W. Fremont National Forest, Lakeview, OR (?), 42-43°N, 120-122°W. (?) following the address indicates that I'm not sure where the headquarters is located; however a letter will probably arrive if addressed: "Headquarters, X National Forest....".

Topographic Maps, scale 1:250,00[0] (1/4 inch equals one mile) of areas of interest. For example, order "Medford NK 10-5". The area covered by each map of this series is shown on our map in dashed lines. Ask for maps which show forested areas in green. Price 60¢ each. U.S. Geologic Survey, Denver, Co 80225 or Washington, DC 20242. Also ask for "Indexes for California and Oregon of 15-minute topographic maps," no charge. The 15-minutes series is smaller scale: 1:62,500, 1 inch to one mile. Geologic Map of Oregon; Geologic Map of California; were 35¢ each, U.S. Geologic Survey. If you are especially interested in rocks and minerals, also write to State Department of Geology and Mineral Industries, Portland, OR, for an index to geologic maps they issue.

We haven't found a good map of vegetation types.

"Climates of the States," temperature and precipitation data and maps for Oregon and California, 25¢ each, U.S. Government Printing Office, Division of Public Documents, Washington, DC 20402.

Sources in Siskiyou Region

Food Staples: Most grains and pulses are expensive in the small cities of the region, when available at all; anyone coming by motor vehicle is advised to bring his supply. Sources are roughly ordered by price: Albers and other feed and grain stores are in most towns of the region, including quite small communities. Not every store has all of the following: *Wheat,* about $4 per 100 pounds. This is soft, white wheat, grown in east Washington or northeast Oregon. It is as nutritious as hard red wheat except for 25% lower protein content. It may not store for as many years. Contains much chaff which can be removed by washing (chaff floats, kernels sink). Boil like rice until soft. Texture is different from rice but boiled wheat is tasty once one gets accustomed to it. (I'm eating it for breakfast as I write this.) Mix wheat about 5 to 1 with beans or peas for better protein balance. *Molasses*, black-strap, 5¢ per pound in customer's container. (Discarded bleach jug is okay.) *Bone Meal*, feed grade, finely ground, as calcium supplement. 7¢ per pound. *Walnuts*, in shells, 35¢ per pound.

Cliff's Farmers Market, 6th St. south of river. Grant's Pass: Beans, red white and pinto, 15¢ per pound (February 1972).

Warehouse Foodstores, 2100 W. 11th, Eugene. Fair prices on red beans and white rice in quantity.

Food co-op, was near 20th and Emerald in Eugene. Most staples, some good prices (summer 1971).

Jorgensen's Dairy, 1300 Court St., Medford. Powdered milk, $33 per 100 pounds.

Walter G. Vail, northeast of Central Point (in phone book, phone first). Honey in 60 pound cans, competitive prices, (high in 1971 due to poor season).

Rogue Gold cheese factory, Central Point; also store on 5th St., Grant's Pass. Often has store returns, ends and seconds, 70¢ per pound.

Lee's Olive House, Highway 199 (on west side), Cave Junction. Most grains and seeds including some exotic ones. Moderately-high prices (brown rice, $1 for 5 pounds).

Field of Merit health food store, Rogue River Highway just south of river, Grant's Pass, (bear left, next to branch post office). Nice atmosphere and many staples but mostly "organic" at high prices (17¢ per pound for wheat). Okay for food-stamp freeks but not for people making do with dollars.

Health food store, highway 99, Central Point. Same comment.

Getting food stamps is a horrendous hassle in Josephine County (Grant's Pass), perhaps anywhere. Requires ID, "residential address," monthly interview at food-stamp center. Not recommended. (Fall, 1971.)

'Sporting Goods' including pack frames, tents, camp stoves, sleeping bags, special clothing. Prices of new merchandise are competitive with most big-city prices; absence of sales tax in Oregon helps.

Hill's Surplus, 6th St. south of river, Grant's Pass. Has polyethylene film, 6 mil was 2¢ per square foot cut, 1.5¢ per square foot whole roll (October 1971), also polyurethane foam, various thicknesses.

Bazar, Biddle Road, Medford.

Pay-less, East F. St., Grant's Pass; also in Medford.

Used clothing, cooking utensils; Salvation Army in Medford, Grant's Pass and many other cities. Good prices but wool clothing, etc. sells quickly. (Goodwill stores charge very high prices; don't donate to them.)

Gasoline is usually 4¢/gallon less around Central Point-Medford than elsewhere in region; usually 29.9¢/gallon, as low as 24.9¢ during 'wars.'

Propane refills: $1.50 for 5 gallon tank at the Gulf or Shell stations on Redwood Highway (199) southwest of Grants Pass. (Most places are $1.75).

Summering in Siskiyou

Suggested minimum equipment (per adult): Polyethylene film, at least 20 by 30 feet, for rain fly. 100 feet polypropylene rope, at least 1200 pound test, and 100 feet of cord, at least 200 pound test, for rigging fly and miscellaneous. 2 by 3 feet by 2 inches polyurethane foam for sleeping pad. Ground cloth, which may be more polyethylene film. Mosquito bar. Cheap sleeping bag or several heavy blankets. Pack frame, plus some sort of heavy bag which can be lashed to it (need not be a regular pack frame bag). (Hills' Surplus, address above, sells an airforce surplus welded aluminum frame for about $9 which we have found fairly satisfactory; molded plywood frames do not stand up well in this climate.) Small cooking stove. A propane stove is better than kerosene (less smell, cheaper) if you have a 5 gallon propane tank for refilling the cartridge. We use "grasshopper" stove sold by Pay-less; refillable cylinder and adapter brings cost to about $15. Vonu cooking with wood requires waiting until night (because of smoke visibility, an overhead shield which can be black polyethylene (to block the light), and some sort of wood stove (an open fire will melt the polyethylene). Unless you are already experienced at this, I recommend a propane stove as back-up and while learning. Dishes can be made by cutting down empty bleach jugs, discarded at laundromats.

Not counting initial equipment costs, maintenance and travel, one can live for as little as $10 per month in summer, by squatting and by eating mostly wheat supplemented with foraging. In a few days scouting you can find a better squat-spot than any we could publish here (since to do so would reduce its privacy). Find a wooded area, preferably on "public land," and look around. We don't recommend trying to meet us, or other vonuans, the first few weeks you are in the region. Meeting would be difficult, for you and for us. And you will probably learn more doing things on your own at first than talking with us. A meeting will be more worthwhile later when we have some experience in common. But do write us and we will reciprocate (sometimes slowly). If we find ourselves exchanging many letters, and things too, maybe we can set up a joint drop to save postage.

For summer fellowship you might try wandering some of the more accessible mountain valleys. You will come upon assorted squatters and campers, from young freeks to old prospectors (at least that was the situation last summer) – interesting people, mostly, though naturally you usually won't see the more vonu ones. Don't hang around the towns – the bludg are hostile to strangers, especially freeks. (One friend got hassled 3 times in 3 days in Grant's Pass.) Nighttime is especially bad.

Of course keep your camp tidy and be very careful with fires, and even if the forest fuzz discover you, they probably won't bother you (at least this was true last summer). If you are still around Siskiyou come winter or return next summer, and if vonu is your Big Thing, let's see if we might vonu better together.

(from VONU LIFE #6, March 1972)

(Editor's Note: Many of the stores mentioned above may be out of business or may have moved. And the prices are of historical interest only. See the Introduction for help in adjusting the prices for inflation.)

A Search – Of Dr. G. and Rayo

We find wilderness vonu addicting; often delightfully so, sometimes painfully so. Several years ago, when we became van-nomads, that lifestyle seemed to offer the optimum combination of isolation and access. We were not content to spend a week or two in that society if we could spend several weeks out of it. As time passed so did some of our hang-ups and we wanted to be further out and out more of the time. Now, much of the time, we no longer live in our van- we can't get it far enough out. But we still use our van for supply/communication trips into that society. And, more and more, those trips are bummers. No, it's not that society is getting worse – we are not beat up, thrown into jail, nor run out of town wherever we show up. It's just that our tolerance for shit becomes progressively lower – keeping up ID (licenses expire, and need a "residential address"); keeping things on and in our van "legal"; worrying about our personal appearance being too freaky, etc.

I really like E's comment about putting one's body and house on the highway..."The small space occupied largely by those guys with the red lights on their cars..." Of course bludg-land isn't just the pavement, it's all the space visible from and easily accessible from highways, streets and roads – i.e., almost all the houses, shops and farms of that society. (A big advantage of van-nomadism over "conventional" ways is not that the pavements are safer than the rest of bludg-land, but that a nomad spends less time on the pavements and in the rest of bludg-land.)

Several years ago, when I was just a sheep-person with illusions of enlightenment, maintaining serf-tags (ID, etc.) seemed trivial. (When one is waist-deep in sewage, what's another turd more or less.) Now these are the most unvonu parts of our lives and are correspondingly unpleasant.

We have some experience with bicycles and don't think they're an answer. A bike means **more** time in bludg-land per trip – **more** red-lighters and other dangerous drivers whizzing by. As for bikes not needing licenses, that is just a liberty (legal interstice), not a vonu (relative physical invulnerability), and probably a short-lived one. Already tax-hungry bludg in California are proposing state licensing of bikes, just like automobiles. (The fees will supposedly go for maintenance of bikeways – big deal!)

Nor are we interested in total isolation (yet, at least). We believe primitivism would mean less vonu in the long run. (Primitive societies run afoul of bludg-land sooner or later – consistent avoidance of something requires some knowledge of it.) And there are too many capabilities/things we wish to develop which require equipment, materials and knowledge out of the other society – technology our society doesn't have yet. But personal travel isn't necessary for import-export. All that is needed (for now) is a way to get parcels and messages in and out – interfaces with the freighting and communication services of that society.

Avoidance of personal travel into bludg-land is not without costs. We must buy a particular part, new, through Sears catalog instead of picking it up, used, at a swap-meet. Nor can we engage in business which requires face-to-face encounters. But these costs are small compared to the savings, at least for us.

This brings me to the "retired farmer with pickup truck" who Adam proposed hiring. It is one thing to get some stuff hauled around once a year. It is something else to get mail/parcels picked up and delivered every couple of weeks, which is what we would like. The latter service requires somebody who is not only reliable, but closed-mouth and in sympathy since he is apt to be hassled sooner or later. There are such people (we know several) but they are few and far between.

Dr. G. and I would probably be happy to pay $4 per trip ($100 per year) for such a service. For $4, someone in that society can not afford to go much out of his way to pickup/deliver at our drop. Even though the retired farmer is sympathetic, he is very much in that society, incurs the "high overhead" (psychic even more than financial) there, and will expect to be paid at that society's going rate. Assuming he goes to town every other week anyway, for $4 it might be worth his while to drive 5 miles out of his way to our drop. This severely limits our base location – a desirable wilderness area is not apt to be within a few miles of the relatively few applied-libertarians we could trust to provide such a service. Even if we find such a combination of person and place, suppose he gets sick or moves away: we must move too or pay much higher fees to somebody living further away.

But, if, say, ten vonuan families or groups lived within a 20-mile diameter area, and each would pay $4 for interface service, that's $40. $40 will hire an applied lib, one day every two weeks – pay for his time and 100-miles or more of driving expenses. We and our drops need not be near his home. Such a service is not to replace long-term storage of supplies we know we will use, such as hundreds of pounds of food staples, but for procurement of the unpredictable items and information – a special part for a new device we are developing, a drug to treat a rare disease, a book.

So, Dr. G. and I are seeking other vonuans who (1) have enough mobility to locate in the same area and (2) have interfacing needs similar to our own – i.e., desire fairly frequent parcel carrying to/from the other society, but do not wish to visit that society more often than once a year (if that often).

Our association needn't be a close-togetherness thing. One needn't approve the way the other combs his face. We can have as much or as little internal trade and personal contact as we want.

Dr. G. and I are fairly mobile. At present we can move our base with less than one month's labor. And we are not hung-up on any particular wilderness spot. Nor is "moving" Vonu Life to a new post office box especially difficult. For climate and nuclear-fallout reasons, we probably aren't interested in any area outside the Pacific Northwest (northern California through southwest Alaska) unless it is outside of North America. And we want to be at least 100 miles away from and upwind of the metro areas of Vancouver, Seattle, Portland and San Francisco.

Perhaps we can first come together in Siskiyou region, then when there are more (20? 30? Families), move to the north coast of British Columbia and find an applied-libertarian with a boat instead of a pickup truck. (There are probably more miles of waterways along B.C. coast than there are miles of roads and streets in California plus Oregon.) Climate and terrain there aren't too different from here – somewhat wetter, only a little colder. More people would be necessary there than here fortnightly interfacing to be economical, since the interfacer would probably travel hundreds of miles.

We are seeking only those with enough vonu-living experience, especially living in relative isolation, to know their own minds. And with savings, or a source of income not requiring physical presence in that society much of the time. If this idea appeals to you, but you are inexperienced, I suggest first trying vonu-living, by yourself, in an area convenient to you.

We already know at least two applied-libertarians in Siskiyou Region who would probably be interested in providing pickup/delivery; the problem is coming up with enough of a market to make it worth their while.

If you think your head is anywhere close to yours, do write. Let us know your experience, present situation and objectives; also thoughts you have about interfacing with that society. This is a long-term project of ours – it probably won't happen in a month or two. So if you first read this many moons from now, chances are we will still be interested if not already coming together.

(from VONU LIFE #6, March 1972)

Report on Progress and Problems

Shelter: Shelter development is still our biggest activity. Our situation the past year: vonu, comfort, convenience, winter - we can have any three of the four but not all four at once; i.e., we can live in vonu and comfort with convenience but not in winter. We can be comfortable and vonu during winter if we forgo convenience to do many things. Etc.

We are still living most of the time in polyethylene A-tents; part of the time in our van. Our A-tent survived the winter with one minor mishap. There was an exceptionally heavy snow while we were away. Snow slid down the poly and piled up at the bottom on each side, bowing in the sides and dragging down the ridge rope. The poly was punctured in a few places by sharp-cornered objects under it but didn't tear, nor did the polypropylene ridge rope (1200 pound test) break.

Other problems with the simple A-tent: cold in cold weather; no insect screening of tent as a whole (we use mosquito bar over bed only); no blackout of tent as a whole (again, we use curtain over bed); reflections from sides which slope south, east or west visible for several hundred yards; fastening of sides must be changed whenever weather changes from wet/cool to hot or back (frequently during spring and autumn); clear poly has a short life in daylight.

Our poly tent has held up almost a year now but little direct sunlight strikes it. We tinted it near the ridge with cheap spray paints for possible ultraviolet protection and for better blending with the surroundings. The paint rubs off easily but this isn't a problem so long as the tent doesn't move much. The paint appears much lighter on the poly than on the top of the can so dark shades should be purchased.

Our lay foam-hut has proven very satisfactory for tasks which can be accomplished in a reclining position such as sleeping, reading, eating, erotics. We slept in it from October through May. With two people inside, temperature rise over outside was about 35°F about six inches above the floor. During warm weather the door was left open, covered only with netting. The 2-inch-thick open-cell polyurethane foam (commonly sold for mattresses) "breathed" well. Even on the wettest days the inside stayed dry though beads of moisture condensed (and kept evaporating) on the outside. This was with two of us breathing inside with all vents closed. (The foam hut was inside the poly tent which sheltered it from rain.) At first we laid the foam hut directly on the plastic ground cloth but (apparently) moisture diffusing through the bottom condensed on the plastic and caused puddles in low spots. Then we built a foundation of boughs a few inches above the ground and ground cloth, which solved that problem. No stiffness was noticed inside. A vent plug, about six inches in diameter, was removed from the top when we used a kerosene lamp inside; the lamp was placed under the vent. Ordinary foam is very inflammable so care is required around fire. We replaced the internal brace (to prevent sagging) with cords to overhead runner-ropes which also held up the blackout trap.

The foam sit-hut is not yet satisfactory. Temperature rise was only 15°F over outside (one person); not enough for work requiring bare hands on cold days. Temperature rise was no greater than in lay-hut (also 15° with one person) even though dimensions were smaller – 4 x 6 x 2 feet versus 4 ½ x 9 x 2 feet, probably because there wasn't a tight fitting at the waist. I had hoped that the warmed air, being lighter, would remain trapped within the hut, but apparently there was much convection. Either a snug waist closure or a bottom will be needed for greater warmth. Already it is difficult to get into or out of, and to pull additional things inside. A tight closure or bottom will increase difficulties.

Foam is an easy and "forgiving" material to work with. A piece not quite the right size can be compressed or stretched into place. A mis-cut piece can be glued back together – a join with the proper foam cement is as strong as the foam. Foam is fairly expensive though – our lay hut consumed over $50 worth.

In winter/spring 1971 we built a small den, intending to use it for a workshop and storage. First problem was condensation. In summer warm air trickles in and cools, relative humidity rises past 100%, and dew condenses on everything exposed. Last autumn I put in a fix, I hoped, and left it alone for the winter. I have yet to learn if the condensation problem is solved because last winter it flooded. The den almost filled with water; the things stored in it washed around some and got wet. For drainage there was a four-inch pipe topped by a one-foot cross section of rocks (covered with plastic to keep finer dirt out). This gives an idea of the flow of water! The water apparently welled up from the bottom. The structure was intact except for some washing near the entrance way. I opened up entrances to the drain some more in case clogging was the problem. Next spring I will visit it again and see if the problem is solved.

But, for now anyway, I'm turned off to completely underground structures too big to be assembled away from site (watertight) and packed in – i.e., much larger than a 55-gallon drum. Not only are condensation and drainage likely problems but much equipment is needed to make a den liveable – artificial light and ventilation at least. And the basic structure must be strong to withstand soil pressure/weight. This results in the structure being heavy. This, in turn, requires that the structure be built mostly of native materials – prefabricated sections would be too heavy to backpack very far – no point having a den if there is a conspicuous vehicle trail leading to it. Volume of our den is about 400 cubic feet. Construction time of basic structure was about 400 person-hours. Materials cost less than $100 – mostly plastic film, cord, pins (nails with heads clipped off), drain pipe, and plywood and glue for entrance. Most time consuming was not digging but preparing timbers: scouting trees which could be removed without altering the appearance of the environment, cutting, trimming, transporting, smoothing or debarking, drilling holes for pins. This was all done with hand tools. The only power tools which would have saved significant time would have been a drill/sander.

I now believe our first den was over-designed with respect to vonu, considering the remote and rugged area in which it is located. I would guess the mean time to discovery (MTD) under present conditions as 2000 years. An MTD of 2000 means that if I had 2000 such dens I would expect about one per year to be discovered by somebody.

We are now working on two types of shelter. The first we call a plinu. (That name has no particular significance.) It is semi-underground, like the shuswap but of different form to provide more light and (hopefully) remain dry in wet climate. After the problems with the den, I am proceeding cautiously. I am only building the basic structure this summer and autumn. If that stands up to winter rains, snows and winds, we intend to complete it and move in in early spring – hopefully early enough to check its insulative qualities. The interior will be insulated from outside air but not from the ground, thus using the ground as a heat source during winter and as a heat sink during summer. Ground temperature a few feet down remains about 55°F during the year around in most areas of this region. I expect the inside will remain about 50°F on all but the coldest days. Our objective is to be able to perform all kinds of work in comfort without an artificial heat source. I'm designing for 50 years MTD.

The second type of shelter is an improved poly tent. Unlike the plinu it is for warm weather use only. It is simpler and easier to construct than the plinu.

We have sent inquiries to many manufacturers and dealers in polyethylene, but have yet to find a source of wide (at least 16 feet) plastic in colors other than clear and black, in quantities less than 5000 feet. A source for Monsanto "602", a clear poly but with ultra-violet inhibitor, is A.M. Leonard & Sons Horticultural Tools, Box 816, Piqua, Ohio 45356. Developed for greenhouse use, "602" supposedly lasts two years in direct sunlight compared to six months for ordinary polyethylene. But a 20' by 100' sheet costs $39 plus shipping, compared to $20 to $30 (West Coast) for ordinary clear.

For general storage we are now using wide-mouth steel drums, in the 10 to 17 gallon range, with tops clamped with circumferential bands. With a good gasket these seal water tight. We store food and other supplies which must be kept dry in 4-mil poly bags within the drums. For long storage I place drums under a small open-sided poly A-tent, similar to A-tent previously discussed but with black poly for longer life. Sides are tied out (as with "summer" tent) for ventilation and snow protection. The tent provides extra shade in summer and rain/snow protection in winter which reduces rusting of the drums and saves contents in case both gasket and bag leak (which has happened with one drum in 20). New gaskets would seal better but I haven't found a source.

General thought on shelter: Build small shelters and have several in an area, far enough apart so that discovery of one is not likely to lead to discovery of others. Use soft foot gear, such as moccasins lined with foam, for travel between them and to water source and latrines, to minimize disturbance of ground. (Good conservation and vonu.) Use hard foot gear (regular boots) only when hiking outside of home area. Advantages of multiple small shelters: many more suitable sites; easier to put under/between trees and bushes with little cutting; not as visible; small structure with few possessions appears less 'permanent' if discovered, less likely to arouse curiosity or hostility. Disadvantages: travel between them, items not always at hand when wanted.

Vonu: We have much less contact with unsavory characters now than three years ago when we were living in a van in Southern California. The improvement is due partly to living in a less populated region, partly to our increasing skills. While living at secluded squat-spots, during the last 18 months three groups have seen our van. Two of these, including the only bludg, happened by while we were parked on "private" land with permission. One object, weighing 50 pounds and worth about $15, was stolen from a stash we had on "private" land (with permission). No stranger has seen any of our camps, even though some have been in relatively accessible areas. No one has molested us personally.

Projects for the next year include warning systems and more tell-tale techniques – the latter to indicate if anyone has been near our shelter in our absence.

The bad guys may be trying harder. But we are getting better at hiding much faster than they are getting better at seeking. It's amusing to read letters from people – "conventional" dwellers, mostly – who delight in telling vonuans about all the things Big Brother will do to stop them unless they join a political crusade or something. Big Brother already has 60 million laws and regulations or so. If all laws were consistently enforced, almost every man, woman and child would be in prison for one or more violations. But Big Brother can only extort so much taxes to hire bludg and build spy devices. And taxes are already to – or beyond – the point of diminishing return. Each additional rule to be enforced means existing rules get enforced less.

Someone has worried because the bludg are talking about "requiring" permits to enter "public lands." To put this in proper perspective, consider that for many decades permits have been "required" to hunt – even small game in most states. How many mountain people have ever shot a rabbit or squirrel (at least)? How many had a permit to do so? How many went to jail or were fined for doing so? Of course there are game wardens and every now and then they catch somebody. The few convictions I have heard of were all on circumstantial evidence: somebody's deep freeze was searched and deer meat was found. No doubt the suspect had invited all his friends and relatives to a vension banquet and somebody talked.

Around Siskiyou some freeks are still using 18th-19th-century methods. Someone walks several miles into the woods on "public lands" and builds a conventional cabin out of trees he cuts to clear a garden. And, so far, the bludg do not even have the resources to find and run off these people. Or perhaps the bludg know that if they start hassling a lot of people, some of the least imaginative will start burning the woods. And that would make many people unhappy including the bludg's superiors – the bureaucracies obtain a large part of their funds by selling timber to lumber and paper companies.

We should not get cocky and careless, of course. I appreciate specific, detailed information on tactics and devices in use or readily available, along with suggestions on how to foil these. I have no use for vague, hysterical warnings. Ways of "fighting back" should be considered. But nothing so foolish as shooting at every bludg one sees, or joining political movements. There are several thousand years of evidence that this kind of "fighting back" only makes matters worse.

Regarding Paul D's concern about super metal-detectors: Rocks do move, around here at least. Not every rock every day, of course. But they get pried out by roots, turned over by bears, washed down hillsides, knocked over by other rocks, etc. About bears: while they can be fantastically destructive they create excellent diversions. One bear in one day will alter the landscape more than will a vonuan in a year, if the vonuan is halfway careful. To obtain food a bear turns over rocks, digs after little ground animals, and breaks down branches on berry bushes. Anyone seriously looking for squatters would need a crew of men and a helicopter, full time, to check out the work of each bear. Or else they must exterminate all bears. Then there are deer, porcupines, pack rats.

Of course, bears don't build fires or use metal drums. So woods-vonuans may eventually have to keep fire and metal under cover, stop using them, or create diversions. Anyone really worried about super metal-detectors can always gather up a few dozen empty cans at a dump and leave them here and there, preferably under trees and bushes in rugged country where a helicopter can't land; also leave a few hanging from trees in such a manner that they will bang together now and then for the benefit of detectors which detect the sound of metal against metal. In one day one person could scatter enough cans to keep a crew with "super metal-detectors" busy for at least a year.

Of course, wilderness-vonu may not be as easy here as it apparently is in "totalitarian" Russia where whole factories are hidden in ravines.

Thanks, Paul D. for lead to non-electric radiation detector. I wrote for further information. Olson has cut the price of their surplus CD detector to $5 plus shipping. Possibly it is not selling well. Their order number is XX-113. Olson Electronics, 260 S. Forge St., Akron, Ohio 44327.

Anyone know of a source for an inexpensive nuclear-war detector? This is most likely a special AM radio receiver which sounds an alarm if most broadcast stations shut down or change frequency. It could be made by interfacing an alarm with the automatic gain control circuit of a radio, but there might be time-consuming problems so I'd rather buy one. Without such a device we might not learn that a nuclear attack was made until days or weeks later, and ingest radioactive fallout we could have avoided.

Back to bears: How can they be repelled from a camp not occupied for two months? We have been using a single strand barbed wire electrified fence. But we have been told this won't stop a bear and so far a bear hasn't come around to test it out. I have thought of saving up urine in bleach jugs, then when leaving, tie these upside down at intervals around the perimeter and adjust the tops for a slow drip. Will urine retain the proper smell for several months? Has anyone tried this?

Power: We cooked on a wood stove made from a five-gallon can when we first moved from a van to a base camp, but we have switched back to propane more and more. Now we only cook with wood on an overnight trip where weight is crucial. We switched back for vonu and convenience. With wood we felt we should restrict cooking to nights and rainy days when smoke would not be visible. But at night fire and any light source should be shielded. Also wood smoke is heavier than air once it cools, flows down hills and along creeks, and can be smelled a long way away. Finally, wood gathering and sawing means more activity near camp and more disturbance of environment.

While propane must be imported, we require little. A five-gallon tank now lasts us 6 months, thanks to techniques Dr. G. has developed. Sprouted wheat and beans are palatable after boiling for a minute or two. For rice or millet, the pot is brought to a boil, and then immersed in blankets or foam to retain heat. One further refinement will be to insulate the sides and top of the pot so that less heat is lost while heating to a boil. And we eat many foods raw.

With maximum use of insulated cooking we might be able to generate enough methane from our own shit to replace propane. Other possibilities: charcoal, generated in large batches in a kiln away from camp; 12 volt electric immersion heater plus insulated pot when we have hydroelectric; solar cooking during summer. I hope to experiment with one or more of these during the next year.

Artificial light we use mostly during winter and autumn – at present a kerosene lamp; during the longer days of spring and summer we go to bed at dusk.

For several years now I have wanted to put in a small hydroelectric system – an impulse turbine or a vane pump (the latter suggested by Skye d'Aureous) driving an automobile alternator. But I've been waiting for a shelter more permanent than an A-tent, since there will be several hundred feet of pipe to lay. Even a small creek will provide enough power for our uses. I would like electricity for a fluorescent light to replace the kerosene lamp, and for some electronic development work. At present we use a small gasoline engine driving an auto generator for battery charging.

Sanitation: I'm dissatisfied with our present shallow latrine system – dig a new hole after each defecation, using the dirt to fill in the old hole – because a large area of ground is eventually disturbed, and because of travel between shelter and latrine. We may experiment with deeper holes plus buckets. Any suggestions?

Food: Our diet has not changed much recently. Most of our nutrients still come from stored staples, especially whole grains, pulses and nuts. From February to August we kept records of stored and purchased foods consumed. Quantities are pounds per person per month. Costs are calculated from most recent bulk prices paid.

Stored staples: wheat 15.8 lbs, 67¢; brown rice 6.9 lbs, 69¢; shelled sunflower seeds 5.8 lbs, $2.27; raisins 4.8 lbs, $1.13; popcorn 4.5 lbs, 52¢; red beans 4.4 lbs, 48¢; walnuts in shells 3.7 lbs, 74¢; millet 1.6 lbs, 32¢; dry milk 1.6 lbs, 69¢; buckwheat 0.8 lbs, 16¢; soybeans 0.8 lbs, 12¢; blackstrap molasses 0.7 lbs, 4¢; sugar 0.6 lbs, 7¢; dry kelp 0.4 lbs, 4¢; alfalfa seed 0.4 lbs, 18¢; dry yeast 0.22 lbs, 16¢; limestone flour 0.19 lbs, 0.3¢; subclover seed 0.18 lbs, 8¢; also vitamin pills and seasonings, estimated 40¢. Total 52.4 lbs costing $8.76 per person per month. We ate generously of sunflower seeds because we had a large stash and didn't know how well they would keep.

Other purchased foods: oranges 6.2 lbs, 75¢; grapefruit 2.8 lbs, 28¢; bananas 3.4 lbs, 35¢; apples 0.3 lbs, 3¢; watermellon 1.3 lbs, 9¢; carrots 0.8 lbs, 9¢; cabbage 0.7 lbs, 8¢; beef 0.8 lbs, 57¢; eggs 5, 14¢; cheese 0.5 lbs, 24¢; canned fish 0.3 lbs, 18¢; buttermilk 0.1 qt, 3¢; ice cream 0.4 lbs, 5¢; margarine 0.3 lbs, 9¢; butter 0.1 lbs, 7¢; oil 0.13 lbs,

5¢; garlic 0.06 lbs, 6¢; pastries 0.2 lbs, 12¢; smorgesborg meals 0.35 meals (1 lb ?) 37¢. Total, $3.63 per person per month. I have listed averages, for comparison, but our actual purchases were irregular. For example, during this 5.6 month period we purchased one 15-pound watermelon and ate it, several days later, all in one day. We purchased meat twice, and each time, consumed it within a few days. Oranges, the most frequent purchase, were bought during five trips, and after each, lasted only for a week or two.

Replacement value of purchased food consumed during this period was $12.39 per person per month. Whereas average expenditure on food, calculated for the entire year, was $22.40 per month. (See next section.) Reasons for differences: stores of staples were increased; trips during the 5.6 month period were few and brief, and included not more than two days in populated areas.

Scavenged foods (from grocery trash bins), guess: fruit 4 pounds; melons one pound; vegetables 3 pounds. We made three big hauls during this period – about a hundred pounds total.

Foraged wild foods, guess: meat, cleaned but including bones, one pound; berries, 0.4 pounds; greens, 0.3 pounds. Many berries were picked and eaten while doing other things.

Dr. Gatherer sprouts alfalfa, sub-clover and buckwheat all year which we eat raw as a salad. Wheat is usually sprouted for a day or two to reduce cooking time and improve flavor and digestibility. Some is eaten raw. For breakfast I usually have sprouted wheat and beans, about 4 to 1, briefly boiled. Dr. G. usually fasts until noon. During the day we have one or more snacks of fruits, nuts, milk, occasionally popcorn. For dinner we have sprouts and any other fresh vegetables as a raw salad, any meat, and a starch food which may be rice, millet, popcorn, or bread home-made out of whole wheat flour we grind ourselves. I often flavor rice or millet with walnuts or sunflower seeds. If there is no meat Dr. G. often makes up a stew out of beans or lentils and kelp plus any cookable fresh vegetables on hand.

The berry we gather and eat most frequently is manzanita (Arctostyphylos) which grows abundantly in many areas near the Pacific Coast, is easy to pick (strip off twigs, separate debris while eating), and is palatable if not delectable thru-out summer. Sometimes we reach areas growing many blackberries, black raspberries or Amelanchier (saskatoon berries) at the right time and in a good season and pick gallons in a few hours. But, except on such occasions, foraged berries are expensive compared to imported fruit, even with our low overhead. On a typical occasion I gathered 9 ounces of red huckleberries (Vaccinnium) in two hours. So, on our infrequent trips to town, Dr. G or I top our load on the return with fresh fruit and vegetables to the maximum weight we can handle.

During the last few months foraged meat has included several mice, one rat, several squirrels, one porcupine, one rattlesnake. The mice and rat were caught in ordinary household-type traps. We began trapping for reasons of self-defense, then decided not to waste the meat. The mice were prepared as Olson's Outdoor Survival Handbook suggests: remove skin and guts, then grind or pound them up, bones and all, into a patty. All rodents taste about the same. Mice are easy to trap in winter and early spring, but not the rest of the year when their food is more plentiful. The porcupine and rattlesnake we just happened upon. The porcupine was impressive until it was cleaned; it seemed to be mostly guts. The liver, though, was big and good tasting. Its muscle meat was tough even after a long boiling. The rattlesnake, killed with a stick, was easy to clean, mild flavored and very bony – time consuming to eat. The only deliberate hunting recently has been done by Dr. G. who obtained squirrels and larger animal. Cleaned weight of small game: porcupine about 3 pounds, most squirrels (grey) over one pound, rattlesnake (two foot) 9 ounces, rat 4 ounces, mouse ½ ounce. Cleaning and pounding up one mouse takes me about 10 minutes, so unless I become more adept, mice are expensive meat.

Nutritionally we prefer small game to deer because we eat it fresh; no preservation problems. We are still using some powdered milk and dried yeast which is probably undesireable for long term good health. In April we resolved to purchase no more meat because of expense, contaminants, staleness and preservation difficulties; so far we have kept to it. On two occasions I went for a period of two months with little animal protein and discovered, toward the end of the period, that I could not do rigorous physical work two days in a row – if I attempted to I felt extremely weak. (I felt okay so long as I worked every other day.) Since I had vitamin and mineral supplements and plenty of calories, I'm inclined to believe I had a marginal protein deficiency. Dr. G. has not experienced this. Our staple diet contains more than recommended minimums of essential amino acids in seeds and nuts. But the human digestive system may not be efficient at digesting protein in the presence of a large amount of carbohydrates (seeds are a mixture). And digestive efficiency varies from person to person.

We have not yet put much effort into trapping; shelter and storage have been consuming most of our time. When we do, probably this autumn, we hope to obtain enough small game to replace dry milk and yeast. Also we will experiment with mini-grow-holes for year-round fresh vegetables.

Finances: Dr. G. and I recorded personal expenditures for a period of one year ending this month. Results: *Food:* $536.42 subtotal, including: dry staples (storable) $365.45; spices and flavorings (storable) $10.65; fresh fruit $48.54; fresh vegetables $11.91; fresh meat, cheese, eggs, fluid milk $58.32; 'junk foods' – store-bought ice cream, cookies, bread, TV dinners, canned foods, candy $17.89; prepared meals (restaurants, visiting friends) $17.86. *Shelter and Storage:* $713.05 subtotal including: materials such as plastic film, foam, rope, cord, drums, nails $452.86; appliances, devices and their parts, including stove, lanterns, pack frame, inverter, traps, etc. $116.34; space rental, mostly for storage $43.24; propane and kerosene for cooking, lighting and occasional heating (van) $21.50; tools $14.61; cleaning and miscellaneous supplies $14.50. *Transportation:* $201.24 subtotal, including: gasoline, including tax $124.06; parts and oil $60.08; licenses and tolls $17.10. *Clothing:* $72.22 subtotal, including: materials thread and needles $26.24; footgear $26.62; other ready-to-wear clothing $9.81; laundromat (when in towns) $9.95. *Communication:* $64.57 subtotal, including: books and magazines $32.67; postage (partly estimated) $15.00; phone calls $10.90; stationary (partly estimated) $6.00. *Other:* $32.82 subtotal including: medical, dental and personal supplies and services $28.95; taxes (federal excise and California state sales tax, not counting gasoline) $0.71; miscellaneous $3.16. *Errors and Unrecorded:* (plus) $3.47. *Total:* $1616.85 for one year for two people.

We were surprised and chagrined at the total – higher than the average for the two previous years. Explanations: We built up stores of staples, shelter material and clothing materials so these figures do not represent one year's consumption. Also many shelter items are (hopefully) durable goods. On the other hand our van and motorcycle are depreciating (but probably won't be replaced). Much of our shelter work is intentionally experimental and therefore scrap-generating so we might consider it a business expense. We are still betwixt and between two lifestyles – van-nomadism and something we are still developing/discovering – which increases costs. Excuses!

Seldom were we consciously stingy. We bought most of the things that we saw or knew of that we wanted, but few things of that society appeal to us anymore. Exceptions: no meat or restaurant meals purchased since April; we bought some new books but passed up others on the supposition we could buy them used, borrow them from friends, or scan at libraries.

We put 4300 miles on a van, including two round trips of 2500 and 800 miles, and about 2000 miles on a motorcycle. Our trips to towns of the area were few and brief but we loaded up on fresh fruits and vegetables when we came back. Most of the junk foods were consumed one several-week stay around large cities – the psychological pressures began to get to us.

Comparing our expenses with those of a traditionalist agrarian family, the Colemans, reported in *Wall Street Journal* and reprinted in The Mother Earth News #11: Per person (counting their two year old daughter as one half): food $268 (us) compared to $200 (them, though they claim to grow 80% of theirs); transportation $101 (us, and we are 'nomads'?!) to $300; tools $7 to $80; shelter (except tools) $350 to $80 (their conventional cabin was completed and land was purchased previously); other $83 to $140. Total, $808 (us) to $800 (them).

While we are interested in developing vonu sources of income, so far we have been more concerned with reducing expenses. If expenses are very low, only a few weeks per year spent in a city will suffice to earn money.

Associations, Attitudes, Objectives: At the moment there are very few vonuans – perhaps several hundred in North America. And these are many different places and different life-styles. Most are not in contact with each other. At times Dr. G and I crave association with more people, not only for economic benefits such as pooling outside purchases and trips but for interaction with different minds. But we have discovered that association with sheep-people or bullshitters only makes us 'lonelier'. Such association is like a drink of salt water to a thirsty man. We much prefer just to be with trees, flowers, birds, brooks – and the few people with whom we share values and goals.

But I don't think this will be a problem for long. More and more people are rejecting the attitudes and roles of the servile society. While only a small minority of the whole population, they number tens of thousands. Some attempt to "turn back the clock" by moving to farms or small towns. But rural dwellers are conspicuously unfree, so those who really want freedom will search in other directions.

A vonuan, to me, is not just someone living in a particular manner. Life-styles may change. A life-style which was vonu 100 years ago may not be vonu today; some life-styles vonu today were not possible 100 years ago and may not be vonu 50 years from now. A vonuan is someone who places a high value on relative invulnerability to coercion – someone for whom freedom is worth a fair amount (though not infinite) of effort, inconvenience, discomfort. To a vonuan, vonu is not just a means to other ends, nor is it an ultimate end – like most qualities of life, and life itself, it is both. A vonuan will choose whatever way of living offers personal sovereignty and will change life-style again and again if necessary.

Although life-style may vary, a vonuan can be identified only by what he does – especially by perseverance over a long period, not by what he says. Words are cheap. This is not to reject ideology. Someone who does not see through the myths of the State will not for long remain vonu, if by good fortune he should become vonu. But anti-state ideology isn't enough.

If freedom were free (more precisely, if vonu were gratis), almost everyone would be free (vonu). But freedom isn't free; it is quite expensive and will likely remain costly in the foreseeable future. Most people presently alive do not value vonu very much. One reason, perhaps, is that during thousands of years of pre-technological agriculture servility had a survival value. During this period conventional farming was the most efficient way of producing food. And it is difficult to conceive of a life-style more subject to coercion than that of the traditional farmer. Not only is he visible and usually separated from his fellow, but "his" home and land are especially vulnerable to attack. Servility was not generally pro-survival prior to agriculture. When North America was "settled," few of the natives, who were mostly hunters/foragers, were successfully enslaved. To obtain obedient subjects the bludg had to bring slaves and indentured servants from the most agrarian societies of West Africa and Europe.

I don't know if servility is due mostly to genetic inheritance, to cultural background or to slave-school training. Most likely it is an interaction of all three. But I don't believe that any amount of "education"   (propagandizing)   will   change   the attitudes/values/intelligence of most adults. Nor do I believe that the majority can be manipulated into a "free society" by some elite of would-be philosopher kings. Such an effort will, at most, only change the rulers. So long as most people can be easily manipulated, they will be manipulated for the aggrandizement of the manipulators.

Traditional agriculture is on the way out. (At the moment quite a number of people are playing return-to-ye-olde-homestead games, but few are producing enough food even to feed themselves.) Barring a catastrophe of sufficient magnitude to destroy technology world-wide, I predict that within a few decades there will be inexpensive, light-weight, mostly automated bio-chemical devices capable of converting most organic compounds into most other organic compounds. Load the hopper with dead leaves or sawdust, insert the proper program, wait a few days, and out comes food wafers which are at least as nutritious and tasty as most of the stuff sold in supermarkets today. Insert different programs and out comes various plastics for construction and clothing. Of course this is just one approach. Maybe I will modify my digestive track to convert cellulose to sugar. Maybe I will develop hardier varieties of traditional food plants able to grow wild with little assistance, as well as more palatable varieties of wild plants. For the immediate future maybe mini-grow-holes are the way. In any case, I don't think that farming is the wave of the future.

With the decline of agriculture, servility loses survival value. Improving communication has the same effect – people will no longer need to crowd into cities or be visible anywhere to work and play together. Consider the potentialities of pseudo-random-noise radio transmission – coded transmission detectable only with matching receivers. Even that institution run amok, the contemporary State, has this effect; it is its most gullible and easily-intimidated subjects who are most likely to be killed in its wars. So I think in the long run, people who place a high value on personal/small group sovereignty will become a larger proportion of the human population.

Vonu, while difficult, is easier now than it has been since the neolithic period perhaps as high as one or two percent of the population, through accidents of heredity and environment, have values and abilities sufficient to achieve it. To become vonu we must disentangle ourselves from those who won't or can't achieve it – reject all "reform-society-as-a-whole" schemes, put aside utopian dreams of world-wide free societies, and get with ourselves and each other – build our vonuums and vonuist mini-cultures.

Possibly I underestimate the potential of existing humans. Possibly most people do value vonu and can achieve it. If so we are more apt to help them become free by becoming free ourselves and showing the way, rather than by joining political crusades. Political reform/revolution/re-education has been attempted thousands of times in hundreds of situations over hundreds of centuries, but at most changes only faces and slogans. Any sort of political movement becomes a contest at coercion and manipulation. Past crusades failed not because of "impure motives," "betrayal," or "defects in philosophy" (why is it invariably *defects*, not the good elements, which come to predominate?) but because of their very nature. Function determines form, means determine ends. The very programs of the State most detested by present "reformers" are reforms-gone-to-seeds of past crusaders.

Dr. G and I did not choose our way of life primarily because we expect a nuclear war or other apocalypse within a few years. While we have considered possibilities of various catastrophes in our planning, if nuclear weapons had never been invented we would probably be living much the same way – perhaps somewhat closer to large cities. Institutionalized coercion – States – is a long-existing social phenomenon; war is only its most dramatic form of destruction. We are striving to reduce vulnerability to all forms of coercion and maximize all satisfactions.

Dr. G and I would like to contact more people with similar ideas, attitudes and actions. If you are not in the region, we invite letters. If you are in the region, let's arrange joint drops at least, maybe meet occasionally. I think the Loose Open Association (as Lan has named it) is the best community model, at least at first. Any closer involvements should come only as people get to know each other over an extended time.

We are now able to provide someone with a food stash, shelter and equipment adequate (most of the time) from May through October. This would be already set up in an attractive, secluded spot – several miles (at least) from any habitation (including other vonuans) known to us. We can bring supplies and mail occasionally (once a month?) to someone who wants to remain completely out of that society for a while. By next autumn we may be able to provide year-round shelter. Our prices are low, or we will barter for services/products we want. Of course don't come to Siskiyou because a few vonuans are already here; hoped-for relations might not work out. Come only if, like us, you evaluate the region as optimum for you.

(from VONU LIFE #9, September 1972)

(Editor's Note: See the Introduction to adjust the prices mentioned here for inflation.)

Epilog: The Disappearance

If you want to get in touch with Rayo after reading the preceding chapters, I'm sorry to say that I can't help you. Rayo disappeared in 1974. I don't even know whether he is now dead or alive. We can only speculate about what might have happened to him. Perhaps one of his underground constructions fell in on him, or maybe he was eaten by a bear. Or he could have abandoned "vonu" and returned to a conventional lifestyle. Or maybe he moved overseas. Or perhaps he just decided that he would be freer if he broke off communication, and he is still out there in the mountains, living free.

If it were anyone else, I would guess that this complete silence over so many years must mean that he is dead. But Rayo is different because his goal always was to become invisible to coercers (meaning mainly Government). He might have come to believe that this required that he become invisible to everyone.

I know of only one tantalizing clue that has a bearing on this mystery – Rayo's last known letter. This is dated February 14, 1974. In it he writes to his correspondent:

> "My thinking has undergone major changes in the last several months on interfacing, 'alternate economics,' interrelations in general...I, too, am becoming very dubious as to the value of all 'libertarian club' involvements...We do not intend to use the 'libertarian club' in the future as an avenue for gaining non-anonymous friends or associates."

Since that time, from or concerning Rayo, no one I know has heard one word, or the least rumor. He has completely disappeared.

A Modern Case Study: Karl & Jahla, Australian Van Nomads

[Editor's Note: The following is the "Our Story" page from Karl and Jahla's website, ComfortablyLost.com. This will give you an idea of their lifestyle, some pictures of their homes-on-wheels, and more. Make sure to peruse the website further and check out their van tour!]

Hi!

This website is created and written by Karl and Jahla. In 2012 we decided that it would be a really awesome idea to travel around Australia together to seek waves, hiking trails, festivals, food, new friends and fresh experiences.

With this idea planted we both started to save money and research our options. In November 2013, after almost a year of searching and extensive research, Karl scored a great deal on our first van; a beautiful white, long wheelbase Mitsubishi Delica L400 4WD van.

With the major purchase of the Delica finalised, the dream was now one step closer to becoming reality. Over the next few months, a lot of time and money was invested into researching and purchasing the best value and most effective upgrades, modifications and equipment that would turn this humble 4WD van into a comfortable, fully-equipped, go-(almost)-anywhere campervan. In January 2014 we both submitted formal notice to our respective jobs that we would leave as of February. This allowed a couple of months to refine and complete the process of building up the Delica, and make it as reliable and comfortable as possible before we left in early April.

The original concept of 'Comfortably Lost' is that we have an off road, go-almost-anywhere vehicle that will be carrying enough food, fuel and water to last a number of weeks away from civilisation if needed. Add to this a secondary battery and solar panels to power all of our devices. We also have all the comforts of home with us, including a large double bed, shower and toilet facilities and a multi-burner gas cooker. We are both free from work and any responsibilities. There was no defined timeline for our trip, we just travelled as long as our money lasted and we were enjoying ourselves. There was no rush to end our trip to return back to work. Essentially we wanted to be able to get as lost as we want and still be comfortable, safe and at our own pace. This is, in my opinion, and experience, the perfect way to travel and experience a country.

We spent almost a year travelling around the southern and east coasts of Australia, including five weeks touring Tasmania. Seeing the opportunity to score cheap flights to Chile, we made the decision to drive back north to the beautiful Byron Bay region in far northern NSW where we could stay with family, work, earn some money, and make our plans for our future trip to South America.

After spending a few months living, exploring local sights, and working in northern NSW, we departed to Chile in May 2015. There we purchased a Mitsubishi Montero Sport 4WD wagon and, with the help of some local friends, we converted it into a go-anywhere camper wagon. With this vehicle we continued the Comfortably Lost mission of travel, exploration and adventure around Chile and Bolivia over a period of four months.

We eventually made it back to Australia in late August 2015 and had to finally face a minor crisis of the financial kind. To put it bluntly the past few years of travel and adventure, coupled with minimal income (self-inflicted due to no desire to work in a serious job) had seriously depleted our financial reserves. We made the decision to 'settle down' for the short term future, cut our vehicle expenses associated with the ownership of the Delica, buy a smaller and more economical vehicle, find some work and save money towards our next adventure(s).

In late 2015 we sold the Delica to happy new owners, and purchased an excellent condition Toyota Corolla wagon after a few weeks of research and shopping around. Karl went on to design and build a light-weight, space efficient folding camper system which was a hybrid of our wood-based folding system in our Chilean Montero Sport and the aluminum-ply system in our Delica van.

After almost a year living in rental apartments and only going on short trips with the camper Corolla, we decided it was high time to hit the road again and escape the absurdly expensive rent prices in Australian capital cities and the day-to-day monotony of full-time work.

That decided, Karl found and bought an excellent condition, near new, low-mileage Mercedes-Benz Sprinter (NCV3 LWB) in early 2017. Our current mission is now planning, designing and converting the Sprinter into a basic, but comfortable, stealthy and liveable 'studio on wheels' that can function as a mobile home and office. The planned features include a dinette/lounge, swivel seats, kitchenette, bathroom (with DIY shower and cassette toilet), raised bed, plenty of storage nooks for food and personal items.

The features for the Sprinter include a dinette/lounge, swivel seats, kitchenette, bathroom (with DIY shower and cassette toilet), raised bed, plenty of storage nooks for food and personal items, underbed bicycle storage on slider trays, grey and fresh water tanks under the floor, gas bottle box, three fan-powered roof vents, a large solar panel array on the roof, and a lithium phosphate battery bank to satisfy all our power needs as we work and travel. See our YouTube channel for a tour of our DIY Sprinter van conversion!

We are also in the process of saving, planning and researching for our next major adventures: Europe and UK road trip 2018, and then North America road trip 2019!

We've resolved to capture and share our experiences over a variety of platforms and media with this build. So please bookmark this site, and also look us up on Instagram and Facebook to stay up to date and see what we're up to! We have recently launched a YouTube channel with tours of our van and information about the setup. Check it out and drop a comment if you would like to found out more about our van or travels.

Karl & Jahla
comfortablylost.com

Controlled Schizophrenia: Why "Celebritarians" Are Glorifying Donald Trump

By: Kyle Rearden

Betrayal is all too common within the activist milieu. This is primarily due to the scourge of not only fake grievances but also the very existence of disingenuous activists themselves. Opposing intellectual dishonesty by pointing out sophistry is not just limited to argumentation ethics, for those who publicly claim to value liberty and freedom deserve to be boycotted and ostracized should they ever compromise on their principles solely due to the winds of political expediency.

Controlled schizophrenia is the mental state of an opportunistic citizen-serf who practices doublethink, yet who still acts in his own best interest. Today, this can be observed in the political crusaders, especially those Donald Trump supporters who voted for Ron Paul back during the 2008 and 2012 election cycles. The question to be answered now is, why are any of the "celebritarians" glorifying Trump?

Throughout the 1960s, Rayo described the phenomenon of controlled schizophrenia. He begins by illustrating how an individual's relative freedom could be conceivably measured:

"…[F]reedom is not a monolithic entity; there are various degrees. But not all degrees are necessarily viable. For most people, I suspect that choice is between predominantly servile (vulnerable) life-styles and predominately liberated (invulnerable) life-styles."

Obviously, Rayo saw this in terms of shades of grey, as opposed to an absolutist black and white perspective. He continues:

"If satisfaction could be plotted with respect to freedom for a large number of people, I think the graph would have a low peak of relative satisfaction around 5% to 10% freedom, a higher peak around 90% to 95% freedom, and wide depression in between."

While not a bell curve by any means, this hypothesis of his suggests that the vulnerability of the population to coercion could be gauged proportionally. Clearly, the relative proportions of those in the 5 – 10% batch vis-à-vis the 90 – 95% crowd is itself a separate educated guess, but for purposes of maintaining realism I will presume that the sheer number of those in the 5 – 10% freedom range to be higher than those in the 90 – 95% liberty curve.

If the freedom outlaws comprise the 90 – 95% portion, then who is in the 5 – 10% segment? Rayo explicates:

> "The lower maximum is exemplified in contemporary society by many a 'successful' Middle Amerikan. He lives 'conventionally' but takes advantage of some of the easier, more obvious loopholes. He pays income taxes but hires a tax accountant to maximize deductions. He registers for the draft but goes to college in hope of being made a technician instead of a target. His mental state is one of controlled schizophrenia. He believes most of the statist myths in which he was indoctrinated yet maintains a modicum of skepticism. He goes to church, or at least accepts their standard of morality, but is not 'above' having a drink at a nude bar. He is largely rational in his work but keeps his rationality compartmented; he does not – dares not critically examine his life as a whole." [emphasis added]

Given that the controlled schizophrenics are those who enjoy 5 – 10% relative freedom, then what advantages do they enjoy that the "wide depression" of the typical American does not? Rayo explains:

> "Although self-maintained schizophrenia leads to unhealthy and unhappy complications, on the whole the opportunistic serf may have it better than his more consistent, more gullible, less self-motivated brother who is drafted and becomes a target – and a paraplegic rotting in a VA hospital, struggling along in a low-paying, high-taxed job with a load of installment debts."

In other words, inconsistency (hypocrisy?) is rewarded by the Establishment in the same sense that George Orwell's Julia character expressed the notion that you can disobey the big rules just so long as you kept the small ones. Rayo further extrapolates:

> "But the opportunistic serf is probably also more contented than the 'non-conformist' who tried to be free in some things while remained servile in overall living pattern. One who is half-free and

half-serf dwells in a psychological no-man's land. He knows too much and thinks too independently to play servile status games with conviction and success, yet remains too immersed in, and influenced by, that culture to achieve success/satisfaction on his own terms. This includes many (not all) 'bohemians,' 'adventurers,' black market entrepreneurs, religious/cultural minorities and radicals of all sorts. A half-and-half life-style tends to be unstable: some go on to more complete liberation; some drift back into, at first, outward conformity, then, acceptance of servile norms; some end in psychosis or early death."

Put simply, there are no half measures when it comes to becoming vonuer (that is, comparatively more invulnerable to coercion) — in this sense, the struggle to maintain and increase one's independence must continue progressively, or else honest failure ought to be openly embraced, but not a sophist ex post facto rationalization that seeks to avoid judging success or failure on its own merits.

Too many individuals begin their path towards liberty with a starry-eyed naïveté that, although understandable, is rather quite deadly; I think that the solution to this all-too-common problem is to inculcate a hard-nosed realism about Leviathan's intrinsic nature, particularly with regard to the reality of democide itself. In order to do this, however, would first involve a stubborn resolve to totally reject political crusading and reformist sophistry alike, so until the oxymoronic "anarchist politicians" are routinely ostracized as a matter of course, then the controlled schizophrenics who now support the Donald will remain with us for the foreseeable future, unfortunately.

What of the freedom outlaws comprising that proportion who are 90 – 95% free? Rayo said:

"The higher maximum of satisfaction is attained by someone with a liberated home-based plus some import-export with the servile society. For him, contact with the State is an occasional annoyance and danger, not a big part of his life; thus he can avoid the psychological paralysis that afflicts so many 'non-conformists.' Compared to the opportunistic serf he may enjoy somewhat fewer conveniences (at present) but is happier overall. On the other hand, he has more than someone living in the primitive isolation presently required for 100% freedom."

This very psychological paralysis is what affects the controlled schizophrenics so totally, and I believe it is the primary reason why as many leading "celebritarians" glorify His Wannabe Majesty the Shiny Rug as they do. Not too long ago, celebritarians decried the War on Terror, the violations of civil liberties (such as the NSA's dragnet wiretapping, which itself was based on phony "national security" due to the alleged Islamic threat), and central banking, but now these very same celebritarians demonize the Syrian refugees (many of whom are Christians) and tacitly acquiescence to the scathing immorality of government war, sounding little different than the neoconservatives and other supporters of George W. Bush's presidential administration.

Alone, this is grounds for freedom outlaws to decry and ostracize these volksdeutchers who advocate the very same government propaganda they used to oppose; if anything, this fundamental change in rhetoric and the divisiveness it has caused within libertarian circles reminds me of the public disputes about the 2014 Ukrainian revolution showing how Vladimir Putin's "libertarians" are little else than well-heeled and domesticated lapdogs for the Kremlin, whether they realize it consciously or not.

Is there anything else to be learned from the phenomenon that is controlled schizophrenia? Rayo wrote:

> "Whether one will be happier as a freeman or as a slave partly depends on the individual. But this choice is not open to most libertarians. Relative contentment in servitude is possible only for those who believe in it; most libertarians are too independent and well-informed. For libertarians the choice is between freedom and neurosis. What became of those libertarians of five years ago who gave up (or never tried) achieving personal liberty? Of people I knew, one is now a Catholic. Another is a Mormon. Another committed himself to a mental hospital. Many are occupied with chronic ailments." [emphasis added]

Again, this emphasizes the significance of integrity and ends-means consistency. What controlled schizophrenics, like those in the anti-libertarian "Libertarian" Party who chose Gary Johnson as their presidential nominee this election cycle, despise more than anything else, is sincerity. The partyarchy refuses to tolerate anyone who (at least, attempts to) steadfastly hold onto libertarian principles, and the same is easily observable with the celebritarians who support the Rug that is the Donald. These two factions are woven from the same cloth of authoritarianism, for should you fail to tolerate either "party" line, you are either a "purist" or a cuck, even if in the latter case you rebuke the social justice equality freaks publicly, as I have.

Going into the future, I think Rayo's observation here is rather apt:

> "Freedom does indeed 'need' more full-time professionals; not collective-movement preachers seeking a coterie of followers, but explorers/inventors/developers of liberated life-ways."

That, more than anything else, is what is causing such a rift between political crusading reformists and freedom outlaws – a fundamental difference in terms of strategy and tactics, not altogether unlike the historical disagreements regarding strategy between the Bolsheviks and the Fabian socialists. A separation betwixt the political means and the economic means of making money, between reformism and direct action, is what truly separates someone like Christopher Greene, Eric English, Alex Jones, and even "anarchists" like Stefan Molyneux, Christopher Cantwell, and Dr. Walter Block from someone like Shane Radliff, Derrick Broze, Kal Molinet, and Larken Rose.

Ignoring this true dichotomy only serves to backslide all the effort that has been placed into shrinking the coercive power of the State. I hold that to be willfully blind to this is to be done at your own peril. These popular narratives about the bombastic self-righteousness of the Trump and Johnson supporters alike that they can do no wrong is prima facie evidence of controlled schizophrenia itself; of course, the Party would have you believe that a "purist" like me is doubleplus ungood.

Samuel Konkin III (SEK3) on Rayo and Vonu: Different Approaches?

By: Shane Radliff

If you were a libertarian/anarchist in the 1960s and 70s, southern California was the place to be. This bustling community was home to many ideological figures who largely developed the theory, and practice, of modern libertarian/anarchist thought.

Two gentleman, specifically Rayo (a.k.a El Rayo) and Samuel Konkin III (SEK3), also called this place home for at least some time, although they never crossed paths. Rayo is lesser-known for his development of vonu, and SEK3 is now well-known for his strategy called agorism.

Vonu, **simply defined**, is the hardening of one's lifestyle to such an extent that an individual could be said to have rendered himself nearly invulnerable to coercion; vonu, itself, is an awkward contraction of the phrase "VOluntary Not vUlnerable." This invulnerability from coercion could be defense from public coercers (governments) or private coercers (criminals).

Agorism, on the other hand, is a revolutionary market anarchist strategy that advocates the goal of bringing about a society in which all relations between people are voluntary exchanges by means of counter-economics, which is black and grey market trading; that is, "trafficking" in products and services which are either illegal, or unregulated and untaxed, but not immoral or unethical.

To put it another way, vonu is defensive, whereas agorism is offensive; much like a duality, they could be used together to mutually reinforce each other, not entirely dissimilar to a two-parent household composed of Mommy and Daddy.

Before diving into what SEK3 had to say about Rayo and vonu, let's first compare and contrast the two individuals.

First, both were wholly apolitical, even anti-political.

Rayo chose to not participate in politics, and even went so far as to coin the terms "political crusading" and "bullshit libertarianism." Mainstream politics itself is collective, and Rayo had a term for that too: "collective movementism", which he was also against. From his other idea of "controlled schizophrenia" from his book, it's safe to conclude that he would clump the political crusaders under that label as well.

SEK3 was against political crusading, as he viewed it as an inconsistent application of means and ends. In New Libertarian Manifesto, he said:

"Worst of all is Partyarchy, the anti-concept of pursuing libertarian ends through statist means, especially political parties." (p. 7)

As far as why they both opposed this anti-strategy, they were very much in line.

Secondly, they were both freedom pioneers and developers of strategies that were outside of the political sphere. They differed in approach, but we'll get to that in a moment.

To keep this brief, the last important commonality is that they both saw the advantages of trading in the black and grey markets.

In November 1965, when SEK3 would have been 18 years old, Rayo published an article in Innovator titled, "Self-Seeking: Ethical Enclave (Black Markets)." He defined this concept as:

"An ethical enclave is defined here as voluntary transactions between individuals who are living under a collectivist government, when such transactions are conducted independent of that government. 'Ethical' denotes the distinguishing characteristic of the participating individuals: an adherence to the ethical principle of voluntarism...And 'enclave' denotes physical emersion within a philosophically alien society."

Sounds awfully similar to agorism, right? More on this later—you're going to want to keep reading.

So, where did these two individuals differ?

To start with ideology first, Rayo was not an anarchist—unfortunately, as we discovered in one of his articles, he saw all anarchists as folks who use retaliatory force against the rulers. From the articles that will be discussed momentarily, we also learned that the individuals in the Free Isles Project agreed upon a nominal State.

Konkin, on the other hand, was an openly-avowed anarchist—nothing else needs to be said on that note.

Next, they differed in strategy—Rayo's interfacing with the public was in the form of newsletters and other such publications; as can be ascertained from his book, he didn't have a whole lot of patience for folks and was more of a hermit.

SEK3 was a quite a bit different though—not only did he openly admit that he didn't pay taxes in a debate with Robert Poole, but he had much more of a public presence—he spoke at conferences, wrote books, and pursued culture jamming efforts, such as the CounterCampaign '76.

It's safe to say that these two individuals' approaches varied drastically on this point.

Lastly, Rayo saw mobility as being crucial. He lived as a "van nomad" for awhile, and then pursued wilderness vonu, both methods containing the option to pick up and leave quickly. He also discussed country shopping and minimalist sailboating, which are more evocative of Hakim Bey's idea of Temporary Autonomous Zones, rather than a fixed geographical locale.

SEK3 was different—as we will get to momentarily, he had some disparaging things to say about vonuists. In one article, he wrote, "As for me, anarchy begins at home."

His goal was to recruit individuals to practice in the counter-economy, and he felt like that was best done through face-to-face discussions and conferences. He also believed that doing so in a permanent (or semi-permanent) location was most efficacious, rather than living as a nomad or "retreating," as he would put it.

All of that said, I'd like to tie up one loose end before moving forward.

In passing, I mentioned and defined Rayo's concept known as ethical enclaves, which is strikingly similar to that of SEK3's agorism.

I initially posited in Vonu Podcast #1: An Introduction to Vonu that it is reasonable to believe Rayo had some sort of an impact on SEK3's formulation of agorism. That said, the day of recording the episode, there was no "hard evidence" of that, let alone any evidence that SEK3 was even aware of this pseudonymous individual named Rayo.

I got a wild hair and decided to scour the "interwebs" for any possible connection—aha! There they were.

From January-June 1975, SEK3 published four articles in the Southern Libertarian Review, mostly in the vein of now-libertarian history, as well as some details on the formation of the anti-libertarian "Libertarian" Party, all referencing Rayo and/or vonu specifically.

1) In his article titled, "Anarchozionism," he discusses the earlier referenced Free Isles Project and goes into some detail about how it came about. SEK3 said:

"The Preform crowd either Browned out or went into escapist trips such as becoming nomads, troglodytes, or wilderness dwellers. They sought 'invulnerability to coercion'—or vonu—and PREFORM-INFORM became Vonulife. Recently it sputtered to a halt, and the paranoia freaks drifted back to civilization."

From that, we can gather that SEK3 was familiar with the vonuans and their goals, likely from the publications themselves. As can be seen, his perception of them was quite gloomy to say the least.

2) He published another article in March of 1975 titled, "Carrots And Sticks," wherein he highlights the achievements of various individuals he's fond of and recommends. He gets to a portion of folks that he is not so familiar with:

"Before I leave Southern Calif., let me not slight anyone, but simply affirm that there are many libertarians I know well enough to exalt but who have not the general fame for their less persistent endeavors (generally due to working for a living, an affliction found rarely on the E. Coast). And there are others of fame that do not enjoy my personal knowledge, such as Joe Galambos, Natallee Hall and Skye D'Aureous, El Rayo and Naomi Gatherer, and Lou Rollins, whose good and worthy efforts will someday earn them a more adept chronicler."

At The Vonu Podcast, our conception of Rayo during the 1960s and 70s is that he was not very well-known—it seems like he was part of an extremely niche crowd, and, if he enjoyed fame, it was not by the popular definition.

That being said, the way SEK3 phrases that last portion is interesting: is it possible that Rayo was more popular than we originally assumed? Were (or are) there more vonuans than we assumed there to be?

Also, have we been wrong in claiming that Rayo's freemate's name was "Roberta," and, rather, it was "Naomi?" Was that the pseudonym beneath another pseudonym that she provided Benjamin Best? A little less significant, sure, but with the sparse information available, unfortunately, I don't think we are the "adept chroniclers" that SEK3 was referring too.

3) For those who are deeply interested in libertarian history, SEK3's article, "Libertarian Strategy (1)," may be of interest to you. Herein, there are two different mentions of vonu, specifically publications. Here's what he had to say:

> "So that we are not condemned to relive it, let's review our history. As of December, 1968, libertarian strategy was directed either toward influence of the conservatives or conversion of the independents. It was wholly educational or retreatist. Robert LeFevre's Rampart College, Leonard Read's FEE, Joe Galambos' FEI, Nathaniel Branden's NBI, F. A. Harper's IHS, and Frank Chodorov's ISI were all educational institutes. The VonuLifers, Atlantis group, and Oliverites were seeking escape. Except for the LIBERAL INNOVATOR's leafletting of the Cow Palace in 1964, no libertarians were involved in a political campaign except as deviationist individuals. Many supported Nixon in 1968, but they were clearly of conservative leanings."
>
> …
>
> "Many libertarians also turned inward with incessant psychology sessions and in-group self-criticism. This was the Movement as reflected in 1972 in, say, NEW LIBERTARIAN NOTES, and which could be pieced together from RAP, LIBERTARIAN FORUM, REASON, ACADEMIC ASSOCIATES LETTER, VONULIFE, FREEMAN, SIL NEWS, PACIFIC LIBERTARIAN, and many local newsletters. "

Regarding the first quote, SEK3 is quite accurate in stating that VonuLifers were seeking escape. Although, Rayo does discuss vonu in cities, he notes that, "I know of quite a few vonuists and libertarians who live [Allen] Humble's way, but I know none who seem to like it for very long."

This is mainly due to the city psychological pressures of the statist-servile society, which is why he prefers "to live far enough back in the woods." Other than that minor point, SEK3 is correct.

The second excerpt is particularly interesting, though. Unfortunately, the only VONULIFE articles I have read are those found within Rayo's book. From that, I certainly don't gather the "incessant psychology sessions" or "in-group self-criticism." Rather, from the entirety of the book, it mainly consists of back-and-forth discussions on strategy, much like a forum or Facistbook thread.

I'm not sure what SEK3 was referring to here, but it's definitely possible that he's correct—until we acquire a library of those publications, we'll just have to take his word for it.

4) This last article discusses CounterCampaign '76, which was a culture jamming effort encouraging people to "Vote for Nobody!," much like the one that took form this most recent election cycle. Sarcastically, SEK3 writes:

"And who could we all agree on without sacrificing our principles? Behind whom could students of Murray Rothbard, Robert LeFevre, Ayn Rand, Leonard Read, Joseph Galambos, Karl Hess, Robert A. Heinlein, El Rayo, Natallee Hall, and Harry Browne unite? Nobody."

On a slight tangent, it is pretty cool to see Rayo's name alongside Rothbard, Rand's and Hess'. SEK3 is definitely right though—sure, a similar foundation of principles was adhered to by most of these folks, but the minor differences weren't as minor as would be perceived by the casual statist observer.

The only solution is NOBODY! So, what's the takeaway?

- SEK3 was familiar with Rayo, even if only through the various publications they both read/contributed to;
- Agorism was likely developed based upon Rayo's formulation of ethical enclaves;
- They differed in strategy, and were both particularly harsh towards those they disagreed with—that said, they were more alike than not;
- The history of libertarianism (even within the last 40 years) is chockful of fascinating details.

In closing, we believe that vonu and agorism go hand-in-hand, and offer an extremely powerful solution to the institutionalized coercion brought about by the State, as well as the non-institutionalized coercion brought about by those private criminal syndicates.

Hell, Rayo even included ethical enclaves (trading in the black/grey markets) as a potential option for vonuans, but more so in pursuing financial independence and tax minimization, rather than the revolutionary agorism set out by SEK3 as a means of abolishing the State; because, remember, vonuans are more than happy to "co-exist" in protracted conflict with the State.

Sure, there are differences, but "we" are all individuals—that is the beauty of vonu—it is truly yours for the making.

Additional Resources

- **The Vonu Podcast**: If you want to learn more about anything covered in this book, I'd highly recommend you check out the podcast Kyle Rearden and I do. In season 1, we covered the philosophy of vonu, season 2 was the practice of vonu, and the current season, 3, is where we develop and update vonu to the modern day.
    - o www.vonupodcast.com
- **Vonu: The Search for Personal Freedom, Number 2 – Letters from Rayo**
    - o www.vonupodcast.com/vonu2
- **Vonulife, March 1973 (Special Edition)**
    - o www.vonupodcast.com/vl
- **Ocean Freedom Notes**
    - o www.vonupodcast.com/ofn
- **Self-Liberation Notes**
    - o www.vonupodcast.com/sln
- **Going Mobile**
    - o www.vonupodcast.com/gm
- **Low-Cost Living**
    - o www.vonupodcast.com/lcl
- **Dwelling Portably [sic]**
    - o www.vonupodcast.com/dp
- **Articles About Vonu**
    - o www.vonupodcast.com/vonuarticles
- **Liberty Under Attack**: If you're seeking out paths to personal freedom, then you need to check out The Freedom Umbrella of Direct Action and the Direct Action Series.
    - o www.libertyunderattack.com/FUDA
    - o www.libertyunderattack.com/DAS
- **The Last Bastille Blog**: This is Kyle's blog and it's chockful of incredible, highly valuable information. He has written over 150 book reviews, a couple books pertinent to vonu, and much more.

- o   www.thelastbastille.com
- **YouTube**: If you're pursuing any of the lifestyle changes or strategies I covered above, then YouTube will be your best friend. Recommended search terms: "van dwelling," "living aboard a boat," "minimalist sailboating," etc.

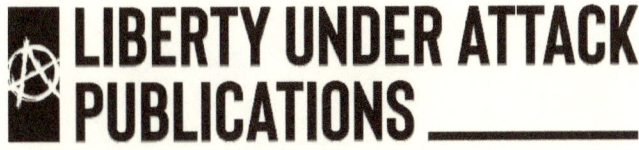

Support Us

If you enjoyed the book and found it valuable, please consider making a bitcoin donation!

Bitcoin: 15Bdzduwt92jYFGFaK2NSkPYFTaLbtonJg

www.ingramcontent.com/pod-product-compliance
Lightning Source LLC
Chambersburg PA
CBHW020320290526
45785CB00007B/2853